JACK CLEMO
SELECTED POEMS

Jack Clemo

SELECTED
POEMS

BLOODAXE BOOKS

Copyright © Jack Clemo 1951, 1961, 1967, 1971, 1975, 1986, 1988

ISBN: 1 85224 052 0

First published 1988 by
Bloodaxe Books Ltd,
P.O. Box 1SN,
Newcastle upon Tyne NE99 1SN.

WITH THE ASSISTANCE OF

SOUTH WEST ARTS

Bloodaxe Books Ltd acknowledges
the financial assistance of Northern Arts.

Typesetting by Bryan Williamson, Manchester.

Printed in Great Britain by
Bell & Bain Limited, Glasgow, Scotland.

TO MY WIFE RUTH

'Love's witness shy
Among my psalming leaves...'

Acknowledgements

This book includes poems from the following collections by Jack Clemo: *The Clay Verge* (Chatto & Windus, 1951), *The Map of Clay* (Methuen, 1961), *Cactus on Carmel* (Methuen, 1967), *The Echoing Tip* (Methuen, 1971), *Broad Autumn* (Methuen, 1975), and *A Different Drummer* (Tabb House, Padstow, 1986). Poems from *The Clay Verge* were reprinted in *The Map of Clay*, together with *The Wintry Priesthood* (first published in the Penguin anthology *Poems 1951*), and a new group of poems, *Frontier Signals*.

The selection was made by Jack Clemo in consultation with Bloodaxe Books, with helpful suggestions provided by Paul Hyland.

Special thanks are due to Mrs Caroline White of Tabb House, Padstow, for permission to include the poems from *A Different Drummer*, which is still in print, and to Lionel Miskin for permission to reproduce the cover portrait.

Contents

FROM THE ECHOING TIP (1971)

FROM BROAD AUTUMN (1975)

FROM A DIFFERENT DRUMMER (1986)

NEW POEMS

FROM **THE MAP OF CLAY**
(1961)

THE CLAY VERGE
THE WINTRY PRIESTHOOD
FRONTIER SIGNALS

FROM **THE CLAY VERGE**
(1951)

A Calvinist in Love

I will not kiss you, country fashion,
  By hedgesides where
  Weasel and hare
Claim kinship with our passion.

I care no more for fickle moonlight:
  Would rather see
  Your face touch me
Under a claywork dune-light.

I want no scent or softness round us
  When we embrace:
  We could not trace
Therein what beauties bound us.

This bare clay-pit is truest setting
  For love like ours:
  No bed of flowers
But sand-ledge for our petting.

The Spring is not our mating season:
  The lift of sap
  Would but entrap
Our souls and lead to treason.

This truculent gale, this pang of winter
  Awake our joy,
  For they employ
Moods that made Calvary splinter.

We need no vague and dreamy fancies:
  Care not to sight
  The Infinite
In transient necromancies.

No poetry of earth can fasten
  Its vampire mouth
  Upon our youth:
We know the sly assassin.

We cannot fuse with fallen Nature's
    Our rhythmic tide:
      It is allied
With laws beyond the creatures.

It draws from older, sterner oceans
    Its sensuous swell:
      Too near to Hell
Are we for earthly motions.

Our love is full-grown Dogma's offspring,
    Election's child,
      Making the wild
Heats of our blood an offering.

The Water-Wheel

Dead wood with its load of stones
    Amid the living wood!
Tugged by the wheel the ballast groans,
    Casts on the little brood
    Of trees its alien mood.

The wheel spins dourly round,
    Wet flanges menacing,
Yet curbed and forced back underground,
    Snarling and shuddering
    Beneath the water's sting.

The iron rods are gripped;
    Tree-high the pulleys slur:
The budding boughs are bruised and stripped:
    Dead iron, live branches blur
    In rhythmic massacre.

The plashy ground turns white
    With clay-silt from the wheel,
And still the trough pours on to smite
    Both wood and iron, to seal
    The dream-world with the real.

Neutral Ground

God's image was washed out of Nature
    By the flood of the Fall:
No symbol remains to inspire me,
    And none to appal.

His Hand did not fashion the vistas
    These poets admire,
For He is too busied in glutting
    The worm and the fire.

Not in Nature or God must my vision
    Now find some relief
While I deepen my hatred of beauty,
    Suspend my belief.

I will turn to a world that is ravaged,
    Yet not by His Will,
A world whose derision of Nature
    Is rigid and shrill.

I have lost all the sensitive, tender,
    Deep insights of man:
I will look round a claywork in winter,
    And note what I can.

Snowfall at Kernick

Here with a burly flutter and sting
    The snow-blast scampers winnowing,
And dribble of foam-flakes seeps and bores
    Through clay-clump thickets, under doors;
While flurry of snow-mist rises where
    The waggons tug till rails are bare.
The smoke is battered round the stacks;
    Soot falls with snow on trolley-tracks.
Even the mica-channel planks
    And narrow walls of settling-tanks
Are frilled and ice-splashed there between
    The frozen pools now sickly green.
The pit-edge merges with the fields,
    A softened gash the clay-bone shields;
Beyond it in the valley's fold
    Virginia woods loom taut and cold.

The Flooded Clay-Pit

These white crags
Cup waves that rub more greedily
Now half-way up the chasm; you see
    Doomed foliage hang like rags;
    The whole clay-belly sags.

What scenes far
Beneath those waters: chimney-pots
That used to smoke; brown rusty clots
    Of wheels still oozing tar;
    Lodge doors that rot ajar.

Those iron rails
Emerge like claws cut short on the dump,
Though once they bore the waggon's thump:
    Now only toads and snails
    Creep round their loosened nails.

Those thin tips
Of massive pit-bed pillars – how
They strain to scab the pool's face now,
    Pressing like famished lips
    Which dread the cold eclipse.

The Cinder-Heap

For twenty years they have lain,
Scorned by the sun and nudged by wind and rain,
Flaky and brittle scabs on mouldering sand.
The whole dune-face is wrinkled with the bruise
Where ash and gravel interfuse,
And the dim clay-land
Cowers in vague watchfulness and fear
As brambles straggle clear,
Pushing with live brown claws
From the hard refuse through the crust
Thrown out by fires long dead: thick rust
Lies on the furnace there
Where the sagging dune-top draws
Slowly around the roofless walls
Of the old engine-house which falls
More ruinous and bare
With every storm that batters. All that's left
Of purging and consuming fire now feeds
The rousing seeds;
And the world of refuse feels the alien sting
In the crumpled cleft,
In the warmth of Spring:
Sap forcing out through rubble, filming green
With soft coarse leaves the gritty silt
Which pit and engine-house have vainly spilt
To make the earth unclean.
And surly in its bafflement
The old black cinder-heap
Confronts the newer dunes on which no brambles creep,
Though they, too, just as bitterly are bent.
This clay-land of the cleansing jet,
The purging fire,
So fears the living sap, the flamy fret
Through stem and vein of earth's desire.

Christ in the Clay-Pit

Why should I find Him here
And not in a church, nor yet
Where Nature heaves a breast like Olivet
Against the stars? I peer
Upon His footsteps in this quarried mud;
I see His blood
In rusty stains on pit-props, waggon-frames
Bristling with nails, not leaves. There were no leaves
Upon His chosen Tree,
No parasitic flowering over shames
Of Eden's primal infidelity.

Just splintered wood and nails
Were fairest blossoming for Him Who speaks
Where mica-silt outbreaks
Like water from the side of His own clay
In that strange day
When He was pierced. Here still the earth-face pales
And rends in earthquake roarings of a blast
With tainted rock outcast
While fields and woods lie dreaming yet of peace
'Twixt God and His creation, of release
From potent wrath – a faith that waxes bold
In churches nestling snugly in the fold
Of scented hillsides where mild shadows brood.
The dark and stubborn mood
Of Him Whose feet are bare upon this mire,
And in the furnace fire
Which hardens all the clay that has escaped,
Would not be understood
By worshippers of beauty toned and shaped
To flower or hymn. I know their facile praise
False to the heart of me, which like this pit
Must still be disembowelled of Nature's stain,
And rendered fit
By violent mouldings through the tunnelled ways
Of all He would regain.

The Excavator

I stand here musing in the rain
This Sabbath evening where the pit-head stain
Of bushes is uprooted, strewn
In waggon-tracks and puddles,
While the fleering downpour fuddles
The few raw flowers along the mouldering dump –
Ridge hollowed and rough-hewn
By the daily grind and thump
Of this grim excavator. It shields me
From lateral rain-gusts, its square body turned
To storm-lashed precipices it has churned.

I feel exultantly
The drip of clayey water from the poised
Still bar above me; thrilling with the rite
Of baptism all my own,
Acknowledging the might
Of God's great arm alone;
Needing no ritual voiced
In speech or earthly idiom to draw
My soul to His new law.

The bars now hinged o'erhead and drooping form
A Cross that lacks the symmetry
Of those in churches, but is more
Like His Whose stooping tore
The vitals from our world's foul secrecy.
This too has power to worm
The entrails from a flint, bearing the scoop
With every searching swoop:
That broken-mouthed gargoyle
Whose iron jaws bite the soil,
Snapping with sadist kisses in the soft
White breasts of rock, and ripping the sleek belly
Of sprawling clay-mounds, lifting as pounded jelly
Flower-roots and bush-tufts with the reeking sand.
I fondle and understand
In lonely worship this malicious tool.

Yes, this is Christian art
To me men could not school
With delicate aesthetes. Their symbols oft
Tempt simple souls like me
Whom Nature meant to seal
With doom of poetry,
And dowered with eye and brain
Sensitive to the stain
Of Beauty and the grace of man's Ideal.
But I have pressed my way
Past all their barren play
Of intellect, adulthood, the refined
Progressive sickness of the mind
Which throws up hues and shapes alien to God's
Way with a man in a stripped clay desert. Now
I am a child again,
With a child's derision of the mentors' rods
And a child's quick pain,
Loving to stand as now in outlawed glee
Amid the squelching mud and make a vow
With joy no priest or poet takes from me.

I cannot speak their language; I am one
Who feels the doggerel of Heaven
Purge earth of poetry; God's foolishness
Laugh through the web man's ripening wisdom spun;
The world's whole culture riven
By moody excavations Love shall bless.

All staining rhythms of Art and Nature break
Within my mind, turn grey, grow truth
Rigid and ominous as this engine's tooth.
And so I am awake:
No more a man who sees
Colour in flowers or hears from birds a song,
Or dares to worship where the throng
Seek Beauty and its old idolatries.
No altar soils my vision with a lax
Adult appeal to sense,
Or festering harmonies' magniloquence.
My faith and symbol shall be stark.
My hand upon these caterpillar-tracks

Bogged in the mud and clay,
I find it easier to pray:
'Keep far from me all loveliness, O God,
And let me laud
Thy meaner moods, so long unprized;
The motions of that twisted, dark,
Deliberate crucial Will
I feel deep-grinding still
Under the dripping clay with which I am baptised.'

The Clay-Tip Worker

Our clay-dumps are converging on the land:
Each day a few more flowers are killed,
A few more mossy hollows filled
With gravel. Like a clutching hand
The refuse moves against the dower,
The flaunting pride and power
Of springtide beauty menacing the sod;
And it is joy to me
To lengthen thus a finger of God
That wars with Poetry.

I feel myself a priest,
Crusading from the tip-beams with my load
And pushing out along the iron lines
My gritty symbol of His new designs.
Creation's mood has ceased
Upon this ribbed height; here He has bestowed
Redemptive vision: I advance to pour
Sand, mud and rock upon the store
Of springtime loveliness idolaters adore.

The tarred rope winds across the mead,
Among the bushes and the weed,
Straight over grooved wheels from the sand-cone's ridge,
Back to the engine-house beside the bridge.
I watch it draw the waggon up the rails,
Smack the surrounding foliage as it whirrs,
Daubing the ferns and furze
Till they droop black and battered, oily flails
Windblown against the turning spokes
Which catch and mangle frond and blossom, bend them over,
Spinning the puffy heads of clover
In dying blobs around the pulley-frames.
And here my faith acclaims
The righting of a balance, a full peace
Slipping from Nature's yokes,
Redemptive truth grey doctrines can release.

This sand-dump's base now licks a hedge
Whose snaky bramble-growths will bear
No flowers or fruit again; a few more days
And they'll be buried 'neath the wedge
Of settling gravel, rotting where
No naturalist may pry to mark their sleep.
The vomit then will creep
Up the sleek boughs of thorn trees that enwrap
The hedge-top, wound and smother them
Till splintered, jammed, they disappear, their sap
Bleeding and drying in the tomb I raise
High over root and soil and mouldering stem.

I love to see the sand I tip
Muzzle the grass and burst the daisy heads.
I watch the hard waves lapping out to still
The soil's rhythm for ever, and I thrill
With solitary song upon my lip,
Exulting as the refuse spreads:
'Praise God, the earth is maimed,
And there will be no daisies in that field
Next spring; it will not yield
A single bloom or grass blade: I shall see
In symbol potently
Christ's Kingdom there restored:
One patch of Poetry reclaimed
By Dogma: one more triumph for our Lord.'

Cornish Anchorite

Deep in the clay-land winter lies my brain,
All faculties that human growth could stain
Dissolved to weedless nescience: here is soil
No poet's pen can scratch, no culture's light despoil.
This vein beyond sap's reach
Teems with no beauties that can teach
My senses mortal joy or mortal pain.
I am exempt at last,
In Dogma's fold till Nature's rhythm be overpast.
I feel a truth the ironic Word has sown,
Truth that draws fibre of human knowledge back
To grey agnostic bone,
Breaks down the nerve of natural piety
To its foul core, turns slack
The muscle of bold self-sufficiency,
And lets the once proud clay
In dumb humility decay.
There is no worship here, only the worm I call
Original sin, and fire of the Fall.
Worm and fire at my roots, how should I know
Your sunshine, song of your birds, you poet brood?
How should I share your pagan glow?
I am beyond your seasons: food
For these is in your blood but not in me.
I lapse from Nature towards a birth
Of Heaven's fertility
That blasphemes Spring upon your earth.

Clay-Land Moods

There squats amid these pyramids
The Sphinx-mood of a Deity,
    Unfelt until He bids
Sandstorms awaken and the choking dust
Drive me across the moors of barren trust.
Then I perceive the aloof grey shape, the scorn,
Quiet veiled cruelty of the watching eyes:
The grim mysterious Will all help denies.
The feet press out until my roots are torn,
Caught by the mauling claws. In silence He
    Smothers and tortures me.

Here on the sharp clay-tip there broods
Olympian thunder, bold and swift,
    Fiercest of all God's moods.
One flash therefrom and peaks of vision seethe
With hostile potency: while wrathful vapours writhe
I creep down rain-grooves, cravenly slink to hide
In caves of the pit, and bruised with panic prayer
Unknown to Mammon's sober workmen there,
I wait till lightnings, thunder-rasps have died
And God allows His terror-mood to lift
    From off the senseless rift.

There is a certain mystic hour
When pyramid and clay-tip grow
    Alive with darker power;
A mood unknown to Nature, a mortal mood
Caught up into His Godhead: taste of blood,
Anguish that makes each tip-frame a gibbet, bared
Until I feel on each the swing of my hand, a pale
Ghost-self of primal guilt that drives the nail.
And the Sphinx-mood is mercy, Olympus tame compared
With my deserts. Then I begin to know
    Why I am tested so.

A Kindred Battlefield
(to T.F. Powys)

Thunder of swinish gods
    And the noontide heat too fierce
Upon the Chaldon clods:
    Yet calmly your eyes pierce

The gross, dank earth and cloud,
    The moody God's disguise,
Wherein His Cross has bowed
    The festering pagan skies.

Wounds in both God and swine!
    The strife of healing breaks
The passive hills that pine,
    The sullen sea that wakes.

White cliffs and goring hail!
    You watch the mystic tide
Lash where no prayers avail
    While soul and sense divide:

Soul seeking the Fatherland
    Beyond the heaven that frowns;
Sense brooding where it scanned
    Dead bones on Chaldon Downs.

This is the battlefield,
    Fluid and undefined:
Land, sea, life, death, revealed,
    Confused within the mind.

A labyrinth, a maze,
    Each chalky Dorset lane:
No landmark steadfast stays
    To guide the questing brain.

The baffling hedge of thorns,
    The swirling mist and sea,
The goblin world that scorns,
    Fret you continually.

Till noontide thunders cease
    And you behold the sign:
Buds potent with release,
    Promise of God's good wine.

Strength for the weary feet:
    Vision of inland heights.
The striving gods retreat;
    You find new paths, new lights.

The homely Stour may tame
    Terrors of Madder Hill,
The new earth name the Name –
    My clay-world feel the thrill.

Chalk heart and clay heart share
    A wilful strategy:
The strife you learned to bear
    Breaks westward over me.

The Two Beds
(to D.H. Lawrence)

You were a child of the black pit,
The grimy tunnellings where fuel and treasure
Are one, and yield to the shrewd blow,
And the stifling air awaits the chance gesture
Which brings the tension, flame and death
In the explosive blast; and the image
Remained with you, a blindness of those deeps
And strange distortions in the hot fumes
Too near the earth's bowels. You never saw
The clay as I have seen it, high
On the bare hills, the little breasts
So white in the sun, all the veins running white
Down to the broad womb with its scars.
And the scars meant, beyond fertility,
Purgation – symbol of the stained rock,
And the live water searching, cooling
Along the bare sinew; and then the heat,
The brief heat beyond the body; and at last
The cup for the new wine. (But that is yonder
And this is faith.) So I had the open view,
While you groped in cramped seams, found no heavenly clue.

But you sought always: all around the world
The one mind bored in the narrow duct,
Straining and twisting for the light, the other warmth
That comes with Springtide of belief, deep, deep,
In plenitude more potent than mere soul.

Could light of my clay have fallen
On your black pit (yet not my light,
But the Light that is not as you supposed;
I tell you, the Man who died
Is not as you supposed), why, then
Your symbol would have changed, flesh have been known
As clay-bed and not coal-bed, its yield
The patterned cup for the great Marriage-feast,
No brute-lump of dusky fuel, soiling, corroding
With its primordial stain as it goes unpurged
From the subterranean womb to fires of perdition.

B

You did not find the true flesh,
Which feeds no fire, though it is tempered
By fires of the Spirit, and does not lapse or swoon
In quest or consummation, nor taste oblivion
In love or death; it knows only
Life more abundant, which means consciousness
Ascending to the All-conscious, finding otherness
In vigour of the new Day, not slipping, gliding,
Fading down the shaft of drugged sense to the dead
Coal-forests where the dark gods reign, silently breeding
The sensual theosophy, the second death.

Epilogue
Priest Out of Bondage

Dark, mutinous land: I shared
Its moods through my dead youth, but I am spared
To wake and live and know it a husk and tetter
Which faith and sunrise peel from my soul.
I slip with every other fetter
The Cornish bond, for I must be whole
Within the eternal Moment, and have no root
In soil or race, in the annals
Of the Celt, or in the dubious channels
Whence idiosyncrasies and tensions shoot.

I rise, no longer dark,
No longer mutinous, and embark
On the journey outward, the escape
To air that is rid of superstition, to a pulse
That draws no heavy blood from the obscure
Cycles of savagery, the historic shape
Of atavism. I shed the lure
Of a dim mother-breast I have outgrown,
And while the Moment's hot fierce joys convulse
My heart I take the irrevocable step beyond
Loyalty to this dead land: no longer bone
Of my bone is its granite, nor flesh
Of my flesh its clay:
The bright blade of the Word severs the barbarous bond.

Christ calls from the tarred road and I must go,
Not as an exile, no,
Nor as one deprived, but as one
Moving to fulfilment, moving home
Out of the ancestral mesh,
Out of the bitter moorlands where my tears
Fell on the sullen bramble and the dun
Rock of the derelict years.
Heir of the Moment and the electing Way
Whence all my treasures come,
I tread in the newness of truth
Where dawn-flushed pylons trample the uncouth

Spells of the tribal night. And this dead land
Which bore and moulded me for a fate
Sour as its soil and hard with its hate
Smoulders and glowers behind the plucked brand
It will never regain or understand.

FROM **FRONTIER SIGNALS**
(1961)

Goonvean Claywork Farm
(to My Mother)

Near the white gashed cliff where the orchard
Held its brave menaced fruit
You crouched and were tortured
By the clang on the thrusting rails,
Watching the iron lines encroach,
Hearing the clash of the buffers
That signalled my fate's approach,
The grimy burdens rumbling through the clay.
You knew how the young earth suffers
And the last harvest fails
In a flurry of sagging soot,
And the fertile faith is an oasis-field,
Hemmed in and peeled
By the blast. But you could pray.

In the sodden ditch beside the line
You wrestled for the healing sign,
Though the orchard had gone,
Cleft through by the blundering blast.
The sweet fruits had gone, and at last
The old home fell to the stroke:
Its grey walls rocked and broke,
And we were left alone.

Stroke at the heart – and yet
There was still a mark of grace:
Though the orchard fell the stable stayed:
To this day it stands with its sweet warm straw,
The black trucks baulked ten yards away.
My desecrating fates invade
So far, no further. You overheard
By the scabbed cliff-face
Among the apple trees,
Only the fanged decrees
Of a derelict Fall
Whose gritty pressure did not daunt my seed at all.

For the stable spoke of an higher Law,
The birth of the Word
Who saw you when your fruit was mown
In the mire, and set
Bounds to the clay-waste, won
A new earth for your son.

Reclaimed

The beams have been wrenched from the tip,
The rails torn from the slope,
And the sodden snout
Poised skyward seems more brutishly to mope:
Just a bald blunt pile in winter's grip;
Flood-waters rising as the dune sags
With dribble of slack sand, pout
Of loosened stone from crumbling rifts,
Where sleepers rot amid the drifts,
And at its mud-white base
The tangled wires are flicked
By the icy wind that nags
At the mass of scrap – old pulley-frames,
The waggon stiff and derelict,
Scarred signal-posts from the sunken face,
And the wooden gangway a girder mains.

I stand alone
On the dark rain-broken cone,
Rejoicing in a kindred nakedness.
My soul once felt the press
Of the iron track of fate,
The rumbling of the refuse-laden hours,
And the pitiless signals violate
My faith as the vomit spilled.
But now the fanged pit cowers;
Baptismal waters flood the bed of clay,
Fate's workings are stilled.
Storm-flash of grace has bared my spirit's peak
And the scabrous flesh grows sleek
Till the young breast, immune and sealed
From fate, lies healed
In dreams of the reclaiming day.

Beyond Trethosa Chapel

It flashed in Cornwall, at Meledor,
My rebel vision, kindling the scarp,
Cutting the bond at my spirit's core.
The Bethel stood in full view, a sharp
Alien scab across the dale,
On the fork of the hill: its lure was stale.
I had wrestled past it in my revolt,
And amid the sand-bruised furze
Was moulding my separate prophecy,
Climbing the ridge with my thunderbolt
To answer the worshippers.

But my hand is stayed; half guiltily
I shelter a hope of peace.
Beyond the gutted memory
Some heart may be ripe and rare,
Reaching to mine with a kindred stress,
Though she lets its flame be tempered – yes,
In the common house of prayer.

Mediate, then, beloved; let tension cease,
Dune-grit and pews be reconciled:
Let not the peak be cut away,
Nor the fold reviled.
Harsh clang of the prophetic tip
May yet be blent, through you,
With hymn of fellowship
My childhood knew.
Bless with your dreams my broken clay
As you take the broken bread;
Fuse the corporate flame with our lonely ray;
Show me that Bethel wine is red.

Meteorite

Faith has some blisses still
That striving flesh may name,
And in the recognition split the heavenly flame,
Receiving to its bed the meteorite
From planetary spaces of the spirit's flight,
Till the elected kiss
Reveals the clay-world oasis:
Sense nourished in the boundaries of grace,
The wayward meteorite grown precious in its place;
And challenging the carnal will
That once controlled our fates,
The cooled core dreams and mediates.

Tregerthen Shadow

(to D.H. Lawrence)

There was a day
When I slept unknowing, an infant here in Cornwall,
And you passed so near, your living breath
Terribly near me, and your shadow
Upon the unconscious seed for the brief touch,
The impress and delineation
Of its stain and flow within the fixed channel
Where yours had fretted and was rousing still,
Ablaze with potency. And the shade
Of your passing was marked by fate, and the mark stayed.

For there were times in after years
When I felt the vague stirring, the bruise
Of the dark unrest around Tregerthen.
It came up with the west wind
And with the amorous mists when the grey peaks
Of my clay-dumps sank to oblivion.
And I felt the chill fear
Lest your end should be mine and a strange god find in me
His way to Isis in her Cornish form, Isis
Of the grit-hard mystery,
Isis of the crag-clotted womb,
And my night-black pit become
A shrine where the unknown god might heal his wounds
In the intimate lapse.

This was my fate, I knew, unless the cleared veins
Of my clay were given back, and the clear skies
Showed the live mood, the untiring purgation
Breaking the natural channel, peeling
Your shadow from the slit cliff.
And the fog lifted, the wind changed course.
I was not deceived in my vision;
I was not for the Celtic Isis or the gods
Of your stricken shade, but for the Word
And white light on the breasts.

Intimate Landscape

Here is the holy ground,
Earth-womb where springs abound,
Some frank for my refreshment, laughing still
If clumsy hand disturb them, others numbed
To poison at an uncouth touch. I thrill,
Sensing these waters yet unplumbed,
Fearful that when I stoop to slake
My thirst I may mistake
Unless you guide and show
Which waters at which hours are mine to know.

Under a smoky sky I view white cones,
Some sharp with ice where fanged revulsions scab
Their bowels, while others mask the tones
Of smouldering volcanic heat;
Yet all are yours, and stab
Alike on casual lover's glance,
And paths along their slopes look similarly sweet
To one unlearned in subtly-hid significance.

Oh darling, lead me safely through the world:
Make clear each sign lest my male clay be hurled
To flame when it seeks cooling, or to ice
When lava leaps in you, hot veins entice
Beneath a white breast I misread,
Thinking it cold, and pass unconscious of your need.
Instruct my nerves in nuance of your smile
Lest clay-springs of your body deep and pure
Pulse out to consummating ardours while
I track dry kiln-beds, miss the lure,
And slink unpurged through stale dust-laden air,
Kiln-rafters darkening on my nuptial night's despair.

Max Gate
(to Thomas Hardy)

No fiery wrestling sent
The scribble of hope's astonishment
Through the dark pines of Max Gate!
You laboured with the unwindowed word,
Blindly submissive, greyly passionate.

Yet I lingered, sensing the ache which spurred
The tired hand onward with its task;
The smouldering thought which dared not ask
For signs of love within the irony.
I know the mood – no more than mood with me –
When chilly apprehension stirs,
And the soul is driven out
From comfort to the wild heath where the furze
Is cruel in winter, stabbing to the veins
Whichever path is taken. It seemed much,
In the festered moment, that your pity grew
Articulate from the touch
Of the thorns, the fallen pine-leaves. But you drew
Back to the negative release,
The closed curtain and the folded doubt.

I found, besides my thorn, another Tree
In the waste-land; I saw the pains
Fate-rooted – no divine caprice,
But alien fangs which the bright grace
Stoops and destroys when the wanderer's face
Turns homeward and the Tree is recognised.

You missed redemption's paradox amid
Those pines; so I had to bid
Farewell to Max Gate, though its strong
And sombre shade lay long
Upon me, half congenial still.
There at your gate I had surmised
How far the Tree may cast its healing thrill
Behind the curtained guesswork, the fear-numbed will.

And in the twilight, looking back
In lapses on my frontier track,
I almost could conceive
That to blaspheme with tears is to believe.

Daybreak in Dorset
(to Monica Hutchings)

It is not my fate that brought me here,
Though this is Hardy's land;
I am beyond my fate's frontier,
And in the realm of grace expand,
Heart truant and confused
With the flooding mystery –
A land so fertile, yet not alien to me.

Was not my language mere
Curt crumbling jargon of mauled rock,
Or purgatorial fire and sundering shock?
Yet the crabbed text grows pale
And I read instead the living litany
Of virgin earth unbruised
Of winding tree-domed aisles of Blackmoor Vale.

Fate-ridden land, in Hardy's view,
Yet every mood I have glimpsed today
On Dorset's face, each passionate hue,
Puts my bleak fate away.

I have seen the moment's fret
When thundery rain half vexed the little Stour,
And then the smile's full play.
As clear sun poured on hills where the sheep fed
And through the thatch-warm villages I sped
Till summer stood serene,
Enfolding me in rich fulfilment, dower
Of Dorset's heart
My fancy long had set apart
In dream-distilled Mappowder.

And I have seen
Fair golden evening drowse on Bulbarrow Hill
And on grey arch and parapet
Of old Sturminster bridge; then, all too soon
Sherborne in twilight cloistered as the moon
In cool strong candour veered from Cranborne Chase.

And in each new discovery, each tumultuous thrill,
There was no place
For fear of shaping scourge, though Tess's frail
Sad ghost might haunt the mind.
I had left my fate behind:

There could be no betrayal
Save in the night of doubt; and stronger, louder
Than the slurred dubiety
Was the voice of faith's new day.

I am purged now
Even of my purgation: the furnace fires
Are hot in Cornwall, and cold is the sand,
But I take the gentler vow
To sun that ripens when the fierce flame tires.

I have shed the scabs of my hard destiny,
I have crossed the frontier, found a living land,
A vision more complete
Because of Dorset's yield, so magically sweet.

Lunar Pentecost

(to Renée Martz)

Scarred stillness of the brooding bone
    In the slow wash of lunar light:
Such was my ghostly kingdom, a dreamer's land
    Which the real heaven had to smite.

It smote with song – just a fire-flake
    That clove a crater in my clay:
God's jazz-drums seemed to thunder
    Where His lava broke away.

There's a roar in the lunar valley –
    No blast with hard rock thudding down:
This is faith's new vein, a molten joy
    Stinging the brooder's frown.

Grim ritual of the isolate self
    Is doomed now, for the flame laps on:
The beating jazz-fire mounts the white skull,
    Enfolds the credal skeleton.

Hot ragtime stains the austere track,
    Bubbles and burns among my glacial clues;
I shall not find the way back
    To the crag's lip and the wintry bruise.

A fire-flake has pierced my silence,
    And a tongue responds – too deep
To be greyly solemn, too sure
    Of heaven's glowing heart to let me sleep

With the sufferer's image, that cold fang
    Of lunar mystery. Now I feel
God's gay eruption is bedrock truth
    Our stoic solitudes conceal.

Beyond Lourdes
(to St Bernadette)

I, too, have waded to mystic ground
Through icy waters; I felt the sharp stones
In my darkened channel, Bernadette.
White fangs leap forward to God's mountain face
From the nagged spirit and numb bones
And a cleft seethes with contact. There's a shrine
Where nightmare yields to shepherding grace;
The brief fold is fenced amid wolfish snows.

A fang struck the rock, you saw the sign
At your wintry Lourdes, and healing flows
Still from your wounds; and yet
In my own pilgrimage I found
That a vision born of pain
Dissolves in morbid rain.

Faith has schooled me further, brought me round
To the secret you may have lost
Through your suffering: heaven's vivacity
In the child world lit by Pentecost.

Its signal burst through the sidewalk throng:
Staccato winds from an exotic sea
Fanned the target heart until it stirred
With ragtime fibre of the Word,
And the poised lips grew strong
For a contact that needs no pauper's garb
No anguish at river-bed, no barb
To fire the shepherding song.

Bernadette, on your bleak verge
You could scarcely dream
How a jazz-throb gives the ultimate purge;
How the Cross bends closer to the neon-gleam
Than to the grim grotto; how a soul unscarred
By mystic snow and border-stream
May flash the healthier vision, spangled and starred.

Clay Phoenix

Is this the end
Of my pilgrimage and battle – the enigma
Of lightning at noon, the quenched wires
On my peak of vision, the glum dunes festering
Amid smoke from pit-head fires?
I am far down in the pit, and blinded
By the ambiguous flash. Where the signals loomed
All is dark. Am I now entombed?

No, for I did not descend
A narrow shaft for my truth.
The bed is still broad, exposed to the changeful sky,
And there's a breeze among the cloisters
Where I grope for the unique transmuted vein
I saw once in the sunshine and shall find again.

I was right to seek that, the bedrock of nuptial sense,
For it is within the mystery inside,
Forever inside the world that lives in God.
The body too needs prophets in the winter,
For spirit's spring runs wild with flamy pledge
Of flesh beyond the mortal moment, the betrayal
And the dust where chastenings end.

Let my peak be smitten, then, I offer still
No sufferer's creed from a sealed gallery.
My soul foreknows its destined thrill
Beneath the ashes and the oncoming moon,
My phoenix-vision rising from the scorched heart.

I shall see the flesh that is clay, the open-cast mine
Where men are not trapped but work with the wind on their faces
And the cold rain stings them away from the sterile swoon.
No pit-props there to sag with the weight of the ego;
No hot salacious smear on the white rib:
Only, when the vein is touched, the signal granted,
Comes the sharp snap of blast
As the agnostic rock is splintered and the barrier passed.

FROM **CACTUS ON CARMEL**
(1967)

Cactus

Starved cactus in mirage-heat
That shows the distant mouth of the maze:
Slaver of the jackal creeping
Past the headstocks where sensual night
Bristled beyond the last globule
Of spilled Zion-light.

Cactus alone in gully sand,
Apart from the common shadow
Of outcasts inarticulate,
Though dreams of the beast's tooth
Shake the rare fibre, the moon-drawn gland.

When beauty steals and betrays,
A slow pulse calls the far progeny
To the level of the bleared back-street:
Cleft palates jabbering imprecations;
Barred windows, sunken bridges – the unguessed
Litter of a pillaging breast.

Warm hill and loosened valley
That welcome the stranger,
Needing the flame, seeding the cactus,
Feeding the jackal on the unborn...
The scabrous issue must forget
How soiled beauties tempt,
Or, at the maturing turn
Where Zion-light dissolves the desert,
Breathe in compassion, soul's roots exempt.

Eros in Exile

Locked grove, lost grove.
Heavy air from mouldering clay-hills
Fills the arbour and threatens the embrace.
Nuptial bud at the lips
Slips back into the natural stream
Which gyrates blindly in the tense wood,
Offering no drink, taking no reflections:
Opaque dull gloss of instinctive waters
Suddenly untransmuted. Male tower, female flower,
Cower in the grey light. Pride of the copse
Drops as the timid hazel-stems
Lift from the thickened brook their soiled catkins.

Errs flesh or soul that the sense of an intruder
Has renewed some primordial guilt,
Turned bride-bank to silt?
Itch and urge, pitch and surge,
Flatten to a confused cry
Now to conceal, now to defy.
Smeared wings flutter but cannot fly
After the fierce dip that evades true contact.

Foiled bud and wing, soiled catkins – and above,
Outside, wooden beams crossed on the clay-hill.
Another cry, a tie with another temple
More deeply penetrating:
By the rivers of Babylon
We lay down but could not love.

Text from the clear springs, the erect tower,
The surging stem:
If I forget thee, O Jerusalem,
Let my right hand forget her cunning,
Let my right hand forget,
Feel only the deadened stream, dead dream.

So we have but lapsed, in truancy,
Just for a moment, to this drab
Stab of mortality.

Bedrock

When the mind is sealed and rusted,
    Like an old stone-mill that cannot grind again,
One does not try to quarry a slab:
    There are no tools left in the brain.

This is strange discipline for the spirit;
    The rational working seems extinct:
No drill or blast – only a hush of torpor,
    An ego submerged, unlinked.

Too tired to doubt, too jaded to rebel,
    I am spared the agnostic thrust,
And the hewn creed is irrelevant
    To those clogged fissures of self-distrust.

Life at sub-human nightfall:
    Weird straggling growths, lost trails,
And a fear that no glint of God's image
    Remains when reason stales.

Then comes an arresting tremor;
    The unbarred instinct is struck by grace
As a playful hand lifts back the bramble
    From my blind groping face.

The blood exults in discovery:
    Though the stone-heaps moulder on
Around the mind's mill, it does not matter:
    I touch a temple at dawn.

The New Creation

If you were nature's child
I could not love you, for I shun
Corrupted trees and flowers which the sun
Kindled in disobedience. Neither wild
Nor tender are the hills, but stained with seed
Still shadowed by the serpent, while
Streams rasp of ancient guile.
Like evil spirits the winds speed,
Or grope like blinded bawds
From brothel-teeming clods.
The hostile sea now slinks from cliffs
Whereon the new Law's hieroglyphs
Pronounce its tides unclean.
All nature stands obscene
In hideous disguise.
No loveliness remains even in the skies:
Hell snickers in the chatter of a starling,
And fleers in each sunrise,
Because one Eastern tale
That makes creation pale
Is known to me and true.
The Christian nightmare holds me, darling –
Creatively, as I hold you.

Now, you are not of these,
Not one with earth and nature's powers,
For He Who fashioned creeds to shame the flowers
Remade you through His stern theologies.
Limbs, breasts and hair were naught to me
Till cleansed by baptism they grew womanly
Beyond the waiting worm,
And opened love's true term.
Your female rhythms, free now from what they seemed,
Surge lonely: nowhere in the unredeemed,
Unconscious heat of beast or natural man
Is this pulsation, hunger, liberty,
This Galilean ban
On weariness and lack
And sad inconstancy

Which follow beast and man at mating call.
The dark waves of the Fall
Rebound from these, thrown back
By witless instinct or by mortal pride.
You only, in my sphere, dared take His side,
His vows that bind,
Submit and know a birth beside His Tree
Which made you lovable, so that you find
You are with child by me.

Bunyan's Daughter

If I could kneel at that grave
In some garrison town – which, I shall never know –
Where you lie, once harlot and slave,
Mother of all my sorrow:
Would the broad skies yield me a drug
Or burn me bare to the debt,
Almost too poignant to be spoken,
Where our life-currents met?

The stinking fens, the chains I hear on gibbets,
The witches' cauldrons – things I'll never see –
Fit the bond between us: fused with a bad dream
Before the dawn-bell summoned me,
You cast the twisted token.

Your practised hand did the routine work,
Pressing the thorns and spear
Into the blind hereditary stream,
Which foamed on through the murk
Till a flesh-clot winced, taking the stab
Under the willows here.

Destined or chanceful target, trapped in ghost-light,
Knowing but speech and sound, shapes warm or cold,
I fled alone, cringing in rain
On spectral cliffs as my hunger woke,
Striving with yours, flung back to a Bedford lane.

I owe to you all the leprous scars,
Peeled deep to slime that spat at the Cross;
Fumes of the sunken furnace,
Ice on the iron bars,
As I staggered from loss to loss,
Hawking laces, bearing the coarse jeer,
Crying all night because you had made me one
Whom pure men would shun.

The world asks questions I do not ask;
My father unlocks the seals

(He was jailed for doing that,
Preaching the answers, hotter than your loin);
And if I meet you at the Golden Gate
The saints will scarcely comprehend
My smile, telling you what a victim feels –
A victim of the traffic coin –
When a parent repents too late.

I would forestall eternity
And let men overhear,
While still on earth, what I have whispered
So often through my tears,
And would whisper again if I knelt where you lie.

I shall reach out to you
With the caress of Christ in my soul till the darkness clears:
Never a condemning thought;
Nor in the end would I undo
All the agony you brought.

I would not insult you with mere forgiveness:
I penetrate the unseen,
Sense something so massive, something so playful,
Mere forgiveness would fall between.

You need not even feel shy,
Dear guard-room Magdalene,
Much less ashamed if we come face to face:
A blight is cancelled, though the smoke of your thighs
Remains till death upon my eyes.

That soldier boy, that camp carouse...
My father dreams of pilgrims now, of grace
So potent at life's core
That he can write: 'I never touched a whore.'

Outsider

You are so civilised, so alert
In your tunnel, arching the drilled brain,
So dextrous in control
Of the tricky signals, the obvious gain.
I am outside, a truant soul,
Deep in the Word, stung by the dirt
Of primal clues which you disdain.

I cannot be a comrade
To you who find your victory
In affliction's craft and trade.
I am angry with your tunnel life,
For a free wind, out here, storms the base
Of resignation, topples the perch of suffering,
Slits like a knife
The bladdered boast, the wan competent face;
And it seeks you also, but you hide from its sting.

I pioneer for you,
But the gulf is too wide
And you cannot see my clue.
I do not have to overcome,
I do not face the worst, I do not accept:
I just speed home
With no flake of darkness admitted or defied.

Your skilled courage is not for me;
I have overstepped,
By God's grace, some mark or boundary
Where faith branches higher
And its vagabond thrills never cool.
I am wild with expectation, full of strange fire
That would scorch a mundane tool.

You miss that fire through your efficiency;
Your triumphs only prove
You are too sleek for miracle. It takes
An unkempt faith to make a mountain move,
Unsheltered savage trust, bare to the mud,

Till your ego's clay-seam quakes
And the Kingdom seethes in your blood.
This fierce old pilgrim's way I have known,
But you despise it, so I sing alone.

Shuttered

I found God's pathway through your touch:
Men call it carnal, but He made it much:
Warm skin and tensed bone seeking
In my male nerve an answering flash,
Till quivering spurts showed quagmires and the rain leaking
Forlornly from the trees that scab the gash
Where the white cliffs crumble, void
Of spirit. But I walked with you
On the narrow track safe homeward while the pent light grew
In the frame unsmitten by the dripping boughs,
Well guarded when the clamorous winds annoyed,
Unharmed amid rocks and sloughs.

I was almost home,
And with you still I would explore
The strange world at my door.
But after the brief lull, the clay-rift prayer
For hope's renewal, you have come,
An alien shell; and my house is bare,
Sharing the blight of the cold vessel,
The lamp more precious than the goal.
Oh whipping memories! Did I wrestle
In vain to keep my treasure whole?

I have no clue to this disguise:
The icy frame, the goring, clanging bone
Which grates mine and recedes unknown
Into the desert mists that rise
And freeze to indifference, apathy,
Between your flesh and me.
I miss the steady jet
Thrown maleward in blithe challenge. Why should you forget
When near my hand again, keen for caressing –
The same hand, eager for the old pressing
To warmth of your blood and strength of the live core,
Freedom and innocence I knew before?

Is it a shuttered mood, apart –
Caprice within the nerve, or passion staled?
I can only wait, with a heart
So vulnerable, trust still for love unveiled.

Exit

Along the railway line that evening,
From the small fenced wharf at Slip bridge
Straight on above the pool to the siding,
Every few steps I scattered farewell words,
Or fragments of them, shred after shred
Torn by relentless fingers, and a dream was dead.
I could not burn that message:
The spurt of flame, the ashes in the cold grate,
Would be too intense an admission,
Leaving scorch-marks like fate.
Better let the sting rot in the mud,
Barred out from my heart's blood.

So I took the stiff card and walked to the wharf
Where the black trucks stood taut and indifferent,
Grimy chains hanging down, buffers silent
As I stumbled past, evading the full blow.
Over the spilled sand-ridge
The sky was tender – scarcely a cloud at dusk.
I saw that no one watched me,
And the hard white flakes began to fall
Between sleepers, into ruts of the path:
And beyond the siding the main line turned away,
Like my heart, towards open clay.

Gulls Nesting Inland

You herring-gulls on truant flight
From sea that roars like dynamite
Find soft blue water, cliffs peeled white.

A cosy world that apes the real,
Where clanging tides can never steal,
Nor salty fangs of spume congeal.

This breeding-ground yields more repose
Than wave-scoured rocks from Looe to Zoze;
But mildness cheats where nothing flows.

I watch you dip your beaks and wings
In water risen from pit-bed springs
That hold no finny shimmerings.

Though you may change your habits here,
You will not see the shoals appear:
No herring feast in claywork sphere.

You are like us who try to school
Our spirits in some sheltered pool,
Fathomed and tideless, never cruel,

Where knowledge bounded and secure
Refreshed us till we shed the lure
Of maddening currents, depths obscure.

But though we choose clay mimicry
Our proper food lies in a sea
Of perilous infinity.

The Riven Niche
(to St Bernadette)

A gilt-lettered phial;
Water from the spring that flows
Where your Lady's feet caressed the rose;
Damp on my brow, the unfathomed sign of the Cross.

Through the moist emblem
I reach to your basilica,
See poplars by the Gave, curved mountain shield,
Small pounding mills
Just clear of the forest; faggots and diadem
On the blind earth where your heaven distils.

The soft Cross of blessing
Is a vision's gift, and the foreign features
Melt to the inner mystery of that gaze
Which you transmit – sometimes half-known
In the scars of my native field.
Barbed truth and blown veil
Blend on the pleading stone.

Before the piercing, on childhood's normal track,
My raw life was so like yours:
Holding my pitcher to the wheezing pump
Or the valley spring-pipe, forty years back.
All waters fouled by clay sores
Around my home, except what the pump lifted
And that clear spurt in the niche
Between bridge wall and thorn-clump,
Where the poisoned brook crawled under the road.

Since then I've heard of creed-crashes,
Of broken moulds and the freedom
Of the unpierced ego to advance alone.
Does your Lady smile,
Or do the swords turn in her heart?
She rebuked the river voices,
Those glib demonic gibes of the passing current;
And now the nuclear wisdom flashes
And trimmed altars await the death-rays.

My spirit moves apart,
Dewy with the new seal, the answering
Unchanged print in the peasant mould.
Riven niche baulks river pride;
And as your baptism spreads I sense the gold
Of blooms on the feet that span the ages,
Fragrance of the wild rose guarding
Multifoliate grace, safe from the slandering tide.

Crab Country

Pincer movement on the hills.
Salty clay-crabs advance, edging sideways
Or straight ahead over fields, lanes and thickets.
The whole scarp slowly fills
With vast crusted shells, gleaming like armour,
And the gravelly claws
Baulk the bus, stop the plough of the farmer.

At night an eye glitters on each humped crest:
The unwinking flares watch the valley –
No stars are needed here.
The eyes have grown fiercer,
Once lanterns, now arc-lights. I sleep
Almost encircled while the crabs creep,
And I wake on shores of protest.

The road to the chapel has been seized
In the new expansion.
Cracked lumps climb and pry
Where the old folk leaned on their sticks
In Sunday spate about their rivered mansion,
And the lovers slipped guardedly by
To stir tides in field gateways.
There too, as I winged to a weekday service,
Birds quivered in their nests
When petrol fumes, dust-clouds from lorries,
Dimmed for a moment the spring hedgerows' glories.

I have known the clay-crabs' tactics all my life,
Been tolerant and made them my symbols;
But I can no longer praise
For the claw-beaten flower, the shell-snapped tree.
Too much of beauty was nipped and slowed
In the intricate strife:
What maimed the bloom has blocked the chapel road.
I am driven to a deeper unity,
A point where sap and prayer,
Seed and creed, tenderly swell,
Sharing the same exemption
From probe of the pincer and crush of the shell.

Confessional

The signals were bannered with surf
And winked blearedly amid the rush
Of pounding ironies.
We were together, but I was bereft
Of clay-bed and hope of tilth
Within my sanctuary's hush.

I knew that this meant contact
More massive than the inland rehearsals.
I had come out to you with just the memory
Of flat clay-pools, a friendly flare on the lip
Between some bramble clumps. But on this outpost strip
We were enclosed, withdrawn
That I might prove my priesthood,
And all familiar images had gone.

Blind trust and blind suspicion
Combed the dark rocks fruitlessly.
My hands traced your damp hair,
But the web was ambiguous still,
For you were voiceless, though the wind was shrill.
True bride or siren – which was crouching there,
Awaiting what ritual, at my feet?
Denied the routine clue,
I stooped for comfort, frail as you.

Then in the swelling kiss
As we submerged, the symbols grew authentic,
The fugitive ego was cleared, baptised.
We were still pent on the shore, but amid the sweet
Miraculous irrigation;
And as my lips ploughed to the crest
I sensed, deep beyond guilt, fecundity
Of rituals yet to be expressed.

Dungeon Ghyll

Rowans – tender, shy, elusive rowans,
Swaying, summer-warm, as a symbol
Of a woman's gift at her nocturnal base:
Soft puffy leaves and sleek stems brushing
Like shaken tresses or the first kiss;
And, with the rowans' whisper, you hear the purl
Of a mountain stream, the pure, blissful cascade.

Here at the foot of Langdale all is guarded:
A flat rocky gulch, a turfed bank for the shy embrace;
But farther up there are rowans, berried so brilliantly
Under the bold green peaks.
And if you ascend to them there is danger;
There might be death, and the resplendent rowans
Would seem to shrug coldly as you fell,
And the torrents would laugh in the moonlight.

Why should there be beauty
On the lip of the ledge where you're tempted?
There could be nettles and a thorn hedge
To keep you safe,
Down at the base, at your innocent meeting-point.

Is the awesome beauty there as a pledge
Of a coronal beyond the shock and the sundering?
Flesh against flesh may chafe
When the wind swoops and blusters;
But suppose you mount the nocturnal height
Sure of rapture, sensing her perfect seed,
And never plundering?

Unberried rowans shadow the path
Where she clings to you still: you must go on,
Up to the blood-red clusters.

Friar's Crag
(to John Ruskin)

Sealed above Derwentwater, I touch the stone,
Sense trees and wavelets, Skiddaw's friendly mass
And Keswick church spire – bland,
Strong as you saw them when you sank, resigned
To the unwedded bone.
You stood here blighted; but a woman's hand
Folds into mine: though our souls have slipped
Somehow apart, my pain
Turns to that spire and not where Brantwood dripped.

How far would you understand,
Who never found the pass
Over the mountains, nor the white-bannered ferry
Fitting the lake-side? Would you frown or thrill
Because, with irony barbed again,
The threat of a dead end
Amid your becks and fells, I still
Have no crushed dream to bury?

I have known so well, in my clay, the stripped
Cold caverns and the misted mind,
But not the burial, when love's chase
Led to the gibbering falls
That filched a face.

This is Friar's Crag; Lodore is near,
Fuming like fate; but the rowans spread
On the exempt ledge, flaunting in the sun,
Though ghostly Rose haunts Coniston.

There is a riddle here
Beyond your shade: even now I am exempt
From the tragic quest, since prayer forestalls
The straining, stinging shocks from the blurred hill.
Faith guards the last rock-bed;
Love finds it tenanted.

Blind above Derwentwater, I feel your stone
Warmed by invisible rays, and am not alone –
Not yet alone.

Carmel
(to St Thérèse of Lisieux)

Gaunt as an ancient dungeon,
Those cloisters of Normandy:
The crucifix raked the unsown breast
Till a breaking lung threw up a blossom
Opening to storm and liberty.

You were the true child-bride,
Burning among the passionless, cold-eyed,
Uncomprehending species, bats or fish,
Who glided in corridors,
Clicked rosaries or tapped a refectory dish.

The chill bell ringing for compline,
Thin nuns' voices chanting in candle-light:
Through such bars of routine
The child-spouse cried of exile,
She-bird pining to match her eagle's flight.

Who are the cheated, who forfeit most?
Not you, Thérèse, but earth-drugged lovers,
Tricked by the unscarred chalice,
Breeding in ignorance of the white host.

Who, tasting the Word, yearns deepest
For the ultimate Carmel of the soul?
Not the frosted nun, but the doubly wedded,
Flesh-fertile pilgrims, canonised at Cana,
Struggling with hints of riper paradox;
Spirits still chaste for Christ, heaven's eagle,
Amid the bedded senses' shocks.

FROM **THE ECHOING TIP**
(1971)

I Go Gentle
(to Dylan Thomas)

That terminal rage gets us nowhere
Except into the wrong grave, the dead end.
My day's light slackens gently
Among these quiet, mystical white horns,
Clay horns that sounded my entry
And are silent only while the clues cohere
For a fuller enactment. I touch a tip,
Feel the echoes, feel the pictures blend
In the bleached cone with no nudge of farewell.
What need of anger as I await the dawn-swell
Of each particle after the lean hour's dip?

My entry was justified
When cloven tongues knit Bedford to Wimpole Street,
Answering my horn;
When taper-blooms bound Mary to the Lourdes foothills,
Answering my horn;
When a Valkyrie's shadow tautened Derwentwater,
Answering my horn;
When a parched face kindled under Weymouth palms,
Answering my horn.

These stirrings were timeless, rising to remake me,
Giving me a voice that rang clear,
A form that wrestled through Promethean myth,
Through fire and bondage, shredding the shams
Till each emerging horn held the true-born
Key and hue. I go with them gently to meet
The unflagging counterpart, beyond death,
Of that creed, that grace of amorous tendrils,
Which your fumings barred from your psalms.

Wedding Eve
(to Ruth)

Chrysanthemums scent the empty chapel
On this last night of my unpartnered bed:
There, foam-like under the dark cliff
Of the pulpit, they blend their stiff
Thick tufts with an unseen swell,
A tide absent when most men wed.

October hush enfolds
The fruits of a creed's battle, of a bond
More real to me than time.
Pews rest in starlight and the hills climb,
Dune-muffled, to this house which holds
The crisp ring and the key beyond.

Elect for marriage – I sang
That stubborn theme through three decades
Of hunger, mirage, avalanche:
When nature made hopes blanch,
A text like a clay-bed tang,
Like the bride's own breath, stirred in the shades.

Forest shade woke you – green boughs,
Fanned sky; then bombers, London's clash,
Splintered your vigil and you fled west,
Prayed under palms and pressed
The white chalk cliffs that spurned the vows
Of your nymph-ardour and dogma-flash.

That Epping trail had to wind
Slowly to my Bethel blooms – no mask
Of dead dreams: tomorrow the grey
Organ-mirror reflects the crowning spray.
Some brides have been tricked, made blind
As they basked, but not where *you* bask.

You chose pure heavenly grace
To mirror the image of your man:
No veiled carnality could pass
The test of that altar-glass;
But it showed you a face, my face,
Scarred, yet singing against earth's ban.

To plant the Cross in the nerves
Intensifies the wedlock sun;
Faith's ravaged fibre now revives
Where the blood thrives,
And I feel in your flushed curves,
In your kiss, the world-renouncing nun.

So two more loves are freed,
Outside an age adrift and dark:
Vigils of dune and forest
Set us on the anchoring quest,
And we find how disenchanted seed
Is changed to spirit's Cana-spark.

The Brownings at Vallombrosa

Not with pagan eyes or the old cloying rapture
  Do they approach that Vallombrosa glade:
A bolder bliss than myth could capture
  Stirs them in the heavy chestnut shade.

Heirs with Christ, their thrill is fiercer
  Than the dryads' ribald revelry:
Creed's communion, though seeming terser,
  Breaks the hot babble of Tuscany.

As they halt in adoration
  The burning text amends the woods' dim scrawl,
And their praise swells for a salvation
  Foreign to the cicada's call.

Lyric currents plough through them,
  Natural as the wild Apennine streams,
And the cultured cynics of Europe view them
  As poets lucky with their dreams.

But back at the Calvinist chapel
  Their subtlest love has leaned to dogma's air:
After the doubts and the maturing grapple
  Came the romantic arbiter.

So unlike their host here, the rigorous abbot,
  Who feels the remote hospice fouled
By a wife's gesture: their stay is short,
  Their vision's not that of the cowled.

What they breathed in Pisa and Paris parks
  They shed now on sanctity and seed –
A rebel grace that marks
  The Puritan juncture at which both are freed.

Drab cells – and earth's beauty grown rank for the wallow....
  But they are risen in Him Whose prophecies shine
On cup and grape till their yearnings follow
  And their pulse redeems the vine.

Leucadian Cliff

The big struggling birds were bound to the victim:
Apollo required the hurled sacrifice,
The plunge of a man, a scapegoat, over the grim
White tusk of cliff; but in mercy or mockery
Strong frantic wings threshed about him.
He might crash on crag or drift gently,
Bob with the birds, afloat
Till dragged into a ritual boat.

No such freak of mitigation
Eased Sappho, the Lesbian muse, at that dropping-place:
No hill-birds were joined to the fallen singer,
No sea-bird strained a pinion
For the illicit voyager.
Art's nectar-tongue had drilled towards the swoon,
And on the swoon's verge a tongue of despair
Split a lifetime's gossamer,
Bared the cheat of supreme pagan grace:
Soon a fire on the beach curled round her sea-sucked face.

Only ashes returned, ashes for a Lesbian grave,
With charred shreds of the bones that had borne her
Under the nightingales and the beguiling moon,
Clutched in her ageing heat, to Phaon's cave –
In the normal trap at last, a lecher's slave.

The tomb of Apollo's servant
Mirrored the broken incantation,
The droppings of her sense-bound song,
Soft fluttering plunge from young violet-scented breasts.
Stealthy fountains had dried in the wrong
Half-light that tricked the nude suppliant
Amid pomegranate, cypress, pine on the sacred hill-crests,
While the Aegean panted the closing bars
Of a death-chant under the locked pre-Christian stars.

Mary Shelley in Geneva

There is a sourness here, not Calvin's fruit,
Nor mere projection of my widowhood.
We found this city, twenty years ago,
Liberal and tolerant to us reprobates:
I an atheist's mistress in my brimming teens,
Suckling a child, Claire bearing Byron's — all
Four of us welcomed, nourished by these shores.
No tap or tinge of Calvin's iron reign,
Nor fate's — except that one dark symbol stirred,
Incongruous prowler of fiction — Frankenstein.

But all has ripened, burst, and I come back
To a sour epilogue of bold ideals.
Mont Blanc is shrouded, ominous and weird,
As if it held that monster of my brain,
Frankenstein's monster, in some clogged ravine.
The lake lies glazed, a swollen Serpentine,
Haunted by Harriet. Is a search going on
For a drowned body? Is there only a search,
Through snow or water-beds, for one's true self
Or a loved one's self, decayed, repulsive, lost?

Why so much irony, sapping, mocking us?
We felt so innocent in our revolt,
Scaling the higher virtue, fertile, free
With the pure earth-gods and the noblest minds;
Read Plato, Sophocles, and watched the moon
Draw lake and vineyard into Shelley's fount
As our boat rocked gently to its moorings. Why
Was each attempt to re-enact that bliss
Wrenched into horror? Think of Lerici:
The grim sea fumbling at our castle walls,
The *Ariel* waiting for the death-trip, I
Driven to miscarriage by my husband's shrieks
When poet's dreams turned nightmares, reason slipped.

I cannot bear these shrill winds and church chimes:
I would loathe religion as my parents did,
As Shelley did, but I am tired, unsure.

I feel we missed some clue, got blinded, trapped;
And what decision would have curbed the blight?
Suppose my father, once in Calvin's fold,
Had broadened the firm core with tenderness
And won my mother to it, brought me up
Believing heaven had chosen me for joy,
High thought and poetry and wedded hearts
Finding a balance in the Christian grace?...
But no: such fancies only cast a smirch
On my imperious memories of love.
Calvin was monstrous. It's my husband's frail
Light I must lean to: I can search no more.

'Torrey Canyon'

One thick black patch, then another,
Pushing coastward greedily
In crude menace that leaks from a gored tanker;
Night's raping crust on the noon sea,
The prance and song of spring waves
Stilled by the belch and stench of that spreading mouth.
Fish die where the poison reaches
Under the floating mounds of oil that soil
Soon the crunched tongues of shingle.

Yet men have said, through bleared piety,
That the wreck of our fuel-laden dreams
Cleanses the soul's tides and beaches...
Oh bright gulls smeared, sinking with grease-deadened screams,
Unwinged in the crash-bred slough!
Fuel-film rotting the seaweed, the smothered cockle;
Rocks daubed, mere slime-heaps, though the rollers' sport
Rinsed them while the tanker ploughed towards port.

In Contrast

The feet that now pause with mine
Where a winter wagtail chafes the stringy twigs
Above the white slow slap of a clay-land rill,
Were wont to pause where Hardy paused,
His nerve drained of desire,
Hearing gulls gabble, wind whip Portland Bill,
And the heart's vultures shriek round a Cornish spire.

The hand which at last lays mine
On the scarp's meek morsels of bride-white hawthorn spray,
Ferns, whortleberries, culled from a sand-cone's lap,
Has reached, as Keats' hand once reached
In febrile flight from love's stings,
Where the sweet Teign dissolves in the red mouth, flap
Of an ebbing sail seems frail as his nightingale's wings.

Harpoon
(to John Knox)

Knox, it was from your seal-sleek,
Eagle-clawed coast that the harpoon winged,
Stilling my fabulous white whale,
Sperm-taut with its spout and plume
Of hot texts, your texts, that scalded
Cool modern currents and shook the minstrel winds
Over untrafficked straits of my clay.

I've been called kin to you who knew
Only the treachery of Mass-drugged queens –
Gay smiles above the saddle, the dirk concealed
That leapt soon at your Kirk's gullet.
For the rest, Berwick moonlight and apple blossom
Flicking Marjorie's face, pledged faithfully,
As Genevan exile proved. You the much-loved,
Never-betrayed husband – how far removed,
As man, from my white whale, speared near harbour,
Harpooned from the pale sands of Skye.

I reach farther back
Into your gaunt story: a black winter at Nantes,
The galley humped like a dark whale
At the Loire's mouth, anchored midstream;
Gale and thong on the stripped Scottish captives,
Clawed from their birthright to the low craft
Laden with loot, moored abroad for their brute death.

A winged mockery struck in dry dusk or at noon;
You threw the Virgin's portrait overboard,
Even with manacled hands, there on that hell-ship.
Your drunken guards had passed it round,
Bidding you kiss their goddess
Who blessed the galley, the floggings, starvation and stench.

You cast away the only grace of colour,
Beauty, charm, for your dour creed's sake.
Nothing remained but the grimy bench,
Bloody chains clanking on hollow skin,
And the untrafficked prayer as you swooned.

Is this a truth for me, for my harpooned
White whale of vision, speared beyond youth?
I cast off the idol beauty
When the ancestral stench seemed all my world;
But only beauty as mute pagan earth
And as man's art, the soft smear you barred,
With your strong thunders, from Scotland's soul.
I never cast to seal or eagle
One image of living face or limb
That spurred my white whale to warmer waters
And its oiled gloss of human sun.

Harpoon means swoon, then richer loveliness
For the miscarried grace, now waking
In prepared currents dear to your Kirk.
The undying texts again plume and spiral,
And my fantastic inner fable
Reshapes in wholeness at a new mouth.

A Couple at Fowey

Swans preen in their white grace on the river;
Clay-trucks are massed on the railway line
That bores past wood-clumps and powdered jetties.
In the wake of our chugging craft
Thin mist scrawls warnings across the estuary:
'Prepare for the swan song, beware
Of the siren's thrumming snare.'
Another white grace, then yet another
Give their protective sign.

Junction in your intent face: we have laughed
At prudence before, and my fused worlds confirm us.
Clay dug where I wept through repulses
Is being loaded now, shipped soon for use overseas,
Or is starting its grooved migrant journey
To Midlands potteries.

How indeed could I be responsive
To nature in her poignant ebbing
Or her cruel fraud? My life runs counter,
Like Browning's in Florence, to this sick process
Of inherent droop and decay. I have known,
Not the young bliss blighted, withering,
But the youthful incubus outgrown;
After fate's clouts, the mature release
From dark tuition, from the coil and harrowing
Of boyhood's unsifted doubts.

Not through me can nature express her sadness;
I have no buried joys, and so my art's
Never a voice for the unassuaged departure,
For the earth's pang which autumn wind asserts
When drained leaves drop and drift here on the cold flux.
Tomorrow an aching sunset may palpitate
On Channel and Gribbin, hint something
About the fading of love's golden rapture;
But it will speak only for men who avoid the crux
That cuts the soul's communion with its first natal state:
If I saw the waning flickers their point would not penetrate.

This is a wry sweet loneliness – to be
A poet without nostalgia, without the negative
Kindling of transience and despondency.

Alfred Wallis

Clash the timbrels, flash the red texts;
Keep the devil's hands off my brush:
It's from the Word I must paint, beside the broken harbour.
I have seen the hot talons
That tore my fingers, cramped the line's fire
When colour poured like blood across the cardboard.

I've reached a crude end, crude and cruel;
And what's the war about, the new dominion
The devil fights under my leaking roof?
I've done mad things, but colour's sane enough;
Yet it brings me to this: this mouldy room,
Just one chair and a table
With my teapot and the blessed Book
And a crust that stays a crust
Till I eat it, breeds no loaves and fishes.

And yet there's miracle: it's in the colour,
Riot of boat-paint on those packing-sheets.
The house walls sag, the sails reel at sunset;
Shrill trumpetings char the smoky port.
And then I'm through, at grips:
Heaven's caught in trance by my watery eyes
And my old body trembles in possession.

I am pursued when the gleam slips
And mocking laughter fouls the quays once more.
My box-lid dries, I'm shattered for my haul,
Some crime against the rules, both ways.
These art-hounds scorn the frenzy of timbrels;
The red-text lassies stare
When my spirit prays in splashed paint.

I wonder if there is a man, a brother to me,
Somewhere in Cornwall, with this outlawed twist,
Half artist, half revivalist,
Trapped in a port or fort, a soul-slum,
Fearing the same knife, hearing the same drum?

Did I hear a pit-blast too, sand-waggons rumbling?
Is he there? Or was it only the sea
Thundering in from God and Godrevy?

St Just-in-Roseland

Roots of bamboo, eucalyptus, palm,
Curl towards buried Cornish saints;
Exotic leaves twang a jungle prayer
Above the river-bed now drained at ebb-tide,
Where boats lounge on mud-banks and wait
For the gurgling inwash from Falmouth Bay.

In the primitive little church
I pause with a hand on the cold
Moulding of an ancient pillar
While my wife plants our names in the visitors' book.
I have fingered some carved pew-ends
And those rough breathing trunks,
Tropical, weird, barbaric,
Stiff and potent in the tilting graveyard.

Symbols teem: I am reminded
Of man's journey, my journey.
An hour ago I passed under clay pyramids
Where conveyor-belts mounted at a switch-flick
With sullen entrails from the scoop-raided bed.

Beasthood has died or fled
From the jungle which obscured the cone of dreams,
White cone, treasured where the mine is open.
That was our sign, but there was sudden jungle,
Gloom of steaming trees, prowl, and howl
Behind the stumbling features:
Lucifer's trick with the unshod prober.

Advance meant fear of the trail ahead
Narrowing to a bone-strewn and braggart lair
Of mental cravings, with the soul's cry unanswered.
But there was a quake, a stillness
In chosen beds and roots and tides,
The rise of an affirmation.

The bright prophetic pageantry
Is valid once more in faith's dawn-solitudes;
Christ's crested pomp, overshadowing
A hunter's loss, spurs the surrendered feet.

My creed-cone is hard as this pillar,
Flashing on the whole march, the whole vista:
The primal fall where veins were savage,
The modern thrust where veins are afflicted,
The altar that shapes a reconciliation –
All are proved, sharpened by a spiced wind,
As my wife steps back to my side.

Mould of Castile
(to St Teresa)

A streak of Sappho, it is said,
Inflamed you, the painted and imperious
Charmer in velvet robes at Avila;
But soon your withered young bones rattled
On convent stones: gaunt postulant,
You had fled, still dead to God, from a goblin-flare.

No mist or dream had softened
The bold Castilian flint: there was sun-glare
On bull-fights and flashing lizards
And the hot black stems of olives, pungent cistus,
Awaiting the shift and shock, an El Greco storm.

Did you waste thirty years
In fighting the sun, flashing out
With a gay jest between swoons and fears
Of those winged visions? Did election dare
Molest your Spanish pride
To that length, fan a fury of love
That soared, bled in the trap,
Lapped a wilful ease, lastly, in brisk reform?

You were ageing, an enigma still,
When your mules arrived at San José,
And a thunder that thrills my flint
In Cornwall now, spread from the wooden waggons,
Filled with your nuns, lurching over calcined plains,
Up primitive mountain-tracks, drifting aground
On river ferries. You and they were bound
For new cells in Elisha's shadow:
Traditional rock like that which my poet-soul,
As wasted and adamant,
Split and gay as yours, descried
Beyond sly bramble, misted kiln
And the dried voluptuary veins.

Virgin Harbour

How deeply, under Calvin's shadow,
Dare I name you – I with no waxen flares,
I the heretic? I go all the way
With Gabriel, up the rocking stairs,
And breathe my 'Hail Mary' over the miraculous harbour.

As soon as the racial charge claimed your body
God's terse rejoinder nested at its core:
I was spun into grace where those two worlds meet.
A free believer's vow must honour you:
Not from incense and litany,
But from my raw baptismal pain
On a cratered hillside, I come to your feet.

There, at your yielding harbour, for me too
Eternity unloaded its veiled
Explosive love that breeds the last fire
Against man's reverent search, religious gain,
In which your Son is admired merely
And your towering nuptials are never hailed.

I bear a wound or two
Of that battle, I the freelance,
Claimed by no church, vexed by no search for ideas,
But deeper in elemental life, aware
Of the exemption and rebuke
From the heart of heaven, in your immaculate glance.

William Blake Notes a Demonstration

As I plodded home over Hampstead Heath
I saw the red scroll darkening
Against their science; I felt the teeth
Of a drilled herded age, the stifling
Earth-rule unkindled, untried
By terrors of Jehovah, terrors of Los,
Mystery of Lamb and Bride,
Burning rose-ray at the heart of the Cross.

I've been plagued enough by Newton,
But the glutted folly will entrench:
A puffed branch dips into smoke –
Or is it a slimy mast with foreign stench
Bobbing towards the Abbey?
I refuse the mind's cold concubine: the Vine
Bends lovingly, but I hear the reasoners croak.

Where's my Jerusalem? That future London
I see in visions now I am near death,
Is not the Holy City: harlots abound
In street, school and pulpit,
And the winding-sheet seems made of protest banners.
A living soul would never seethe
With that sullen cramped revolt, uncrowned
By the thorn that will make me die singing.
Catherine, I'll die in song: you trust my prophecy;
And I tell you, next century will bring
These soured hollow shapes, and I attest
That heaven's red scroll mocks such peace-planners.
If men can't die praising God
They're not ripe for life, not fit
To protest against the means of exit.

Those marchers, fretting where I once trod,
Should kneel, then create, not glumly sit.
The street they deaden seems intact,
But a poisoned, splintered world looks out
Already from eyes that fear a fire-burst.

Death-rays of pride and cynic's doubt
Were not banned in time and the hard
Revolving ego has been blighted first.

They've missed an apocalyptic fact
Elijah told me and a child-heart understands.
The angels that thronged my garden tree
Will guard the – what's the jargon? – missile-sites,
And the red-scroll's horrors won't cremate the West
Till those angels and their cohorts quit
And the undammed Judgment smites.

The angels would not quit while creators pray;
Judgment won't smite while prodigals plod home,
Stirred by the shining tiger, the hot palm-sign;
But every earth-bound act,
Denying my visions – denying, Catherine,
Robert's ascension and his clapping hands –
Will weaken the spirit-guard,
And the planet slips nearer doom
When rescue bids are made (I see the scene sway,
Fading now) from the shell of the soul's decay.

Katharine Luther

It will be an enchanted night
Heralding your fiftieth birthday, Martin.
The stars swarm thick and blue in the dry air
As the autumn evening softens Wittenberg.
We look through the monastery window
Towards the unruffled Elbe that rubs
Along sandstone banks, low hills, white
As dead wolves' bones in the forests.
The black dog won't haunt your bed
Either: I replaced that nightmare
Eight years back, crowning your conquests.

You struggled this way, sometimes begging bread,
For nearly two decades before I was born.
First the wood-cutting, then the smelting of iron:
I can see the trees snap and lie
Quivering under your father's axe;
I can see the hot furnace, molten ore,
And the finished tool which cracks
So many dark doors. Life meant slash and fire
And wolves' teeth: thus God marked you out
Into ripe manhood without my love. I wonder why?

I missed the great hours of your mature fight –
Never saw you nail that paper
To the door of our Castle church,
Nor Leo's bull turn to ashes at Elster Gate;
I pined in my cell while your cry at Worms shook Europe.
But all your thuds and thunders
Against Tetzel, Duke George, the Pope,
Woke me at last, bludgeoned my barren vows.

You play the lute now, sing,
Serenade me with your hymns and carols;
But it wasn't a gay path we trod to marriage.
We were sober, deliberate – not a prick
Of the florid fervour poets write about:
Unpractised, banned, we knew no amorous trick.

You only sought my hand
Because Melanchthon urged you to choose me
Out of the nine nuns who had fled
From the convent at Nimptsh. We came here,
High-born ladies, in dirty waggons,
Homeless and terrified,
Needing husbands. You even tried
To fix a marriage between me and Glatz!
The personal choice seemed a small thing
Amid faith's awesome warfare, the blazing stakes,
The charred rules by the Tiber.

Yet love grew personal, Martin, it went deeper
Because it served faith and not appetite.
Few people guessed why my wedding ring
Was embossed with emblems of that Death you preach.
The sun's eclipse, the thorn-barbs, spear,
Nail-pocked wood in the earth's quake and swell –
These Passion-signs were drawn within
The bond of our blood. This ring – see,
It's my stigmata, meaning death of a sort,
Heralding a new order of sainthood:
Death within which I bear you children
And the golden caress blooms in the grey cell.

After Billy Bray

Sunday evening on the clay-tip.
A bristle from the far west,
Carn Brea monument, pricked between shoulders
Of sagging white mounds that messed
The approach to chapel walls, pew varnish –
No longer my shrine: iron raspings
Preached to me, tar leaked from a tip-frame axle
Too heavily daubed but relieving the soul-stings.

Down in my home a brass lamp
That once lit the Bethel would glow again
In winter, sharpening my clotted page
As I struck back blindly through memory's rain.
By that lamp's flare I had seen converts cluster
Where the holy wine was kept;
But not a sip remained to stir rhythm or rapture,
Nor a sparkle to show me how he leapt,
Billy Bray the miner, shouting:
'Life and death have lost their sting:
Picked for heaven (Hallelujah!),
I'm a King's son and I will sing.'

The moors of Kea lapsed into dolour
When that dancing figure tapped its last reel
And the merry wit of the troubadour
Ceased to echo around the mine-wheel.
Owls glided towards modern moonrise
Over the Baldhu grave where he slept,
And Twelveheads thorns housed the gaunt rooks
Where his bubbling airs had swept.

I sensed the advance beyond his Kingdom,
The subtle strut without the song:
Our gay Franciscan feast was ended;
The enquiring mind had proved it wrong.
I felt the bristle, I was betrayed
In the new rising of a sunless search.
The owls, the rooks, the chilly light
Drove me up to the clay perch

Where I fashioned the mystic's answer,
Blent Haworth, Geneva, Lourdes
With the lost song of the Cornish miner,
And found my poet-world restored.

Billy Bray (1794-1868), an illiterate tin-miner,
was Cornwall's only notable evangelist.

On the Death of Karl Barth

He ascended from a lonely crag in winter,
His thunder fading in the Alpine dusk;
And a blizzard was back on the Church,
A convenient cloak, sprinkling harlot and husk –
Back again, after all his labour
To clear the passes, give us access
Once more to the old prophetic tongues,
Peak-heats in which man, time, progress
Are lost in reconciliation
With outcast and angered Deity.

He has not gone silenced in defeat:
This suffocating swirl of heresy
Confirms the law he taught us; we keep the glow,
Knowing the season, the rhythm, the consummation.

Truth predicts the eclipse of truth,
And in that eclipse it condemns man,
Whose self-love with its useful schools of thought,
Its pious camouflage of a God within,
Is always the cause of the shadow, the fall, the burial,
The smug rub of hands
Amid a reek of research.

The cyclic, well-meant smothering
Of the accursed footprints inside man's frontier;
The militant revival,
Within time and as an unchanged creed,
Of the eternal form and substance of the Word:
This has marked Western history,
Its life's chief need and counter-need,
From the hour God's feet shook Jordan.

We touched His crag of paradox
Through our tempestuous leader, now dead,
Who ploughed from Safenwil to show us greatness
In a God lonely, exiled, homeless in our sphere,
Since His footfall breeds guilt, stirs dread
Of a love fire-tongued, cleaving our sin,

Retrieving the soul from racial evolution,
Giving it grace to mortify,
In deeps or shallows, all projections of the divine.

The Islets

(to Emily Brontë)

You might have roamed Penwith moors
From a rectory gate above the Channel cliffs:
Warrior eyes stabbing the sea-trapped Mount,
Probing past turret and soft enchantment,
Across the bay, your hot clenched spirit
Intent on lonelier nuptial crests
Where ebb tide never restores
A safe path back to mainland interests.

But the cold North bore your body, fed your soul;
Penwith was spared the searing scrutiny.
Decades slipped by till, forty miles
Nearer to Haworth, I strove on granite stiles.

It was not the flesh-flaw, not your crumbling lung
Or drain of sight and sound from me,
That marooned us where unseen messengers
Fashioned an art from obscure mutiny.
Given the fit frame, we would still
Be driven to covenant and vigil, naming
Clue for clue, flash for flash,
Cornish blood stung by heaven's lash.

The tradition stayed polite
Where your mother felt her heart burn
As she bade farewell to the sleek Mount
And the salt smooth sands of safe return.
On the cultured mainland
The polished masters came and went,
Leaving the correct frail monument.

But on our vision-islets
A mystic storm reshaped the love-shrine,
Dread forms of evil and the divine seed
Emerging on each kneaded crag,
Slag-black, upthrust from the pagan sea-bed.
Those stumps of stubborn faith, distorted carvings,
Defy the rational mainland's preen and sag.

FROM **BROAD AUTUMN**
(1975)

Broad Autumn

True faith matures without discarding:
All I unearthed, each sky-sign crudely mapped
On the white rasped hills of youth,
Warms me still by rowan-tapped crags
Far up the autumnal mountain,
Incredibly remote in climate, texture, weathering
Of bare stones, from my first insights:
I left no wreckage on those low rasped cones.

There is no snarl of tools
Where broad wisdom calls across the cordial heather,
But the hacked glints my young heart stored
Still tone the subtle comforts and the sharp
Fearful shifts of shade as the blood cools
To admit, and clarify, the expanding mental range.

No pestilence of proud ripeness,
Urbane, agnostic, cankers the wide braes
Which my spirit, eagle-keen now, calls native
In the pale sun's gloss. The spikes of raw praise,
Sparse once on the white hills,
Glow ruddier here against the thinned
Thieving of the schooled foreign crows.

I have not changed my country;
I have grown and explored
In my faith's undivided world.
I discard no primal certainty, no rasped
Sky-sign of the Cross;
But now in broad autumn, feeling a new peace
And the old poise of defence,
I accept the pure trysting lochs,
The full antlers in the glens.

Helpston

I never heard wild geese
Nor sowed wild oats, but the omen
Was there like Clare's, straggling from the fen.
This homeless freak, the artist,
Seems born marsh-magnetised
In some Helpston, between bog and limestone,
Distrusting the hard contours, the creed's release.
Reed-fingered swamp and black peat belt
Make the first rhythms bubble and the frontiers melt.

With moonrise on the weird dykes
Comes an ache of expansion to the soul apart,
So nakedly aware,
Amphibious, sensing illicit freedom
Which the fenced herd dislikes.
Banned fancy ventures with the snail,
Grows webbed in shadow where the frogs croak
And swan's wings, goose wings, beat through mist,
Flying low and spectral, back to a watery nest.

There were fields amid Clare's fens;
Peat-land was turned to wheat-land by skilled drainage;
Dykes rose, blurred daily by farmhouse smoke.
Spring's throb and dreams of harvest,
Soft dreams Clare drew from cowslip and pilewort,
Looked clear of slime, and he sought to enclose
In this delicacy the kissed mouth and foam of hair,
The lover's plea for young breasts held bare.

*John Clare, Northamptonshire's peasant poet, was born at
Helpston in 1793, and was buried there in 1864 after spending
nearly thirty years in an asylum.*

Merely instinctive, merely natural,
Unchecked by limestone creed, the greed
Grew: gay love pleaded too often
And a rare beauty was hurt,
Coarsened by tavern stench worse than the bog's.
The white plough-horse trod too deep in the furrows
Of his broken ideal, and his Helpston –
Unlike mine, which choice of limestone saved –
Dropped to the softening water
Till High Beech madhouse hid the crater.

Asian Girl in Mid-Cornwall

Temple darkness – oh, send temple darkness,
Vishnu, Siva! Memories should be golden,
Jewelled in soft dusk, my racial stream
Broad and brown, turbulent after monsoons;
But I've been barred and choked by the press
Of hostile climates. I look back
On African heat and steam
Which turned the brown charms black,
Raw and frightening. Now I'm flung to England,
Hard and dry in cold lights: no balm or spices
In these winds that sting the clay-mine dunes.

What's in my blood that this foreign tang
Poisons? The long centuries' beat
Of ritual drums at temple festivals,
When the brown tide lapped low and Siva's fire
Was raised through the girls' bought bodies,
Anointed lotus-buds, wedded to wisdom,
Shielding the snake's fang, the death of desire.
Initiates in the shrine, mystical swoons
In temple darkness…oh, how it calls
By contrast with this drab Cornish street!

Silken and lovely behind
The temple towns, green forests teem
With banyan and tamarind,
And wild pineapples lean their pink spikes
Over mountain pools and torrents;
Bright birds and beasts glide and mate,
Vibrant with the temple's secret.

My land waits – jewelled, magical, soft in caress –
While I hear Christian bells, the West's wan mode.
Not a pulse here to reclaim me,
Outcast amid horrors – dead white scabs
On ugly hills, miles of them. I see
Engines with teeth, and evil rays at night
On high cones where men unload
Their clanking monsters; and it's all done
As a life's whole key, untouched by temple rite.

Divanie's light – the proverb in India:
Siva's least-loved wife, served with a glimmer.
But even that seems too painful here
In this grim alien zone.
Send temple darkness – utter temple darkness
Now that the chant of mystery finds no echo,
Now that the machine-world of their West
Reviles my prostration.
Dream-drums, wed me quickly
To some kind god, oblivion.

In Harlyn Museum

I am back in the eerie room
After nearly half a century's wash and wear –
A survival myself, an exhibit
More vocal than these relics from a tomb.
I feel the ancient air
Thinner now, drawing no menaces
From the intact flints and human splinters.
Outside, in the imitation burial garden,
Slate cists look mellow under the soft boughs.

When I last stood here
My childish eyes were wide, fear-clouded,
Vaguely mocked by the skulls and bones
Lodged in their neat glass cases.
A tide within me groped among stones,
A chilly friction whispered:
'Ancestors, Celts, before Julius Caesar
Sent his legions towards the Tamar.
Something called death, and then,
After a long spell, something dug up
From Harlyn strand.' I preferred it
To ball games and sand-castles on the beach.

Taste for the blanched root,
For morbid candours in an ultimate twilight,
Scarcely stirs on my return; the mature outreach
Is curious but compassionate, holding faith's fruit.
My wife breathes with me in the charnel-house.

We question together, our feet still tingling
From the Atlantic swirl on shingle cleared on graves.
What deities were worshipped
Inside the delicate white curve
Of that girl's skull? Did she tramp inland,
Perform weird rites on the knoll
We call Brown Willy, her dark breasts stripped
In frenzy at full moon?
There where the blank jaw-bones grin
Her lips were wrenched in shrieked incantations
On the moor, in woods and cliff-caves.

They were pressed out for love too, fierce, untrusting,
As the live skull bore the loose veil of her hair
To her captor's face and shoulders.
Bride and mother, tribal whore, priestess –
Whatever her role here in the bay,
Those sockets held a slave's eyes,
Nagged by fire and wave-break on the hut floor.
Often there was bruised, blood-dripping skin
Around those bones. Did her head lie inert
As hunter or fisher slunk away,
Leaving her raped amid furze or seaweed?

Pagan gods, blood-tides groping
Among crumbled stones, flesh hurt
In the unholy lover's hand.
But after Caesar the joyous saints
Prayed where her skeleton lay, a triangle
Of slate at its mouth, in the dumb sand.

Where shall we strike a balance
Between compassion without hope
And a hope so intense
That no compassion is needed?

Porth Beach

Is it Orual's roll
Or Psyche's bowl I carry, treading barefoot
Back from the outgoing Atlantic tide?
We have passed from loose breaker-bruised sand
To dry tight grain, warm and friendly;
But a myth-pattern chafes and twists
In this Cornish cove, stabbing the holiday
With a foreign and wintry question.

I have just bowed over gleaming breast-high rocks,
Where my love showed me a myriad mussels
Massed on the granite, full of the sea's life,
But closed and reticent in their blue-black shells.

No open voice answers, none relevant
To the myth-frame of my inner journey.
If only the mountain eagle would appear!
If only the kingly bird would cry a decision!
Choughs and gulls alone fly here,
Black or white spies from low cliffs, screeching,
Scanning me with mean local eyes.

I dimly recall the hunt and wounding;
I knew the roar of a landslip, the descent
Into an underworld where I lay almost pulseless
For ten years. But when I struggled back
I brought something strange, unseen, intangible,
A heart-weight of destiny.
I bore it to the altar of wedlock;
I bore it just now to the dripping rock
Where my love showed me the crowded shut shells.

Was it Orual's roll, filled by acid fingers,
Accusing the First Cause? Or did I bring
Back from death's river, in blind trust,
Psyche's level bowl, the unspilt mystery,
The uncompromised surrender?

My love's pressure laps the rigid fear;
Our limbs tingle, drying in the sun:
Soon we shall climb the hill to the field-path.
But even there I shall carry
The unknown token, the question will still tease.

May the judging eagle's verdict
Be merciful to my love:
May the kingly eye see the bowl and the balance
Held daily, the seditious roll
Rotting under the landslip, never my possession.

Testament

(to Joseph Hocking)

Genesis mixed: your Terras tap on clean tin
Foreign to me, though your birth-bed
Was only a mile from mine, the hacked hills
Around us carried the white scriptures
Of a sullen trade, the black Bibles were pounded
In Wesley's fold to make us akin,
And your family blood reached me, according to legal files.

But my craggy and uncouth image
Came another way: Knox-souled and Burns-hearted,
How could I take the sleek service
And the tidy text? My genesis
Was spelled in the scummed saddlebacks
Lolling towards the blasted circle,
The whipped fingers of rock on the pit-floor,
Hoisted hoses making their impress
On rinsed and haggard cliff-faces that wore
Slowly away, starting up at smoke-lidded stacks.

Brute tools broke me in the riding stillness
Of infancy, then the loping waggons,
Glum and fast on the drummed tracks,
Woke me each morning, along with the brayed
Or shrieked summons of engine-house sirens.

My boyhood's dream crossed a mineral stage
Without lark's song or bowing myrtle,
But always with an unbegreyed
Gesture apprehended, God's and woman's
Blood-leap – not in your mild pattern
Of the clean sheet and Victorian climate,
But storming to my unwritten page,
Anguished for all the lost Edens.

Neither the hint of mineral
Iron nail in the Godhead, nor the shuttle
And prick of moon-change in the bride,
Could check the released heart's witness

116

That nightmares abate, that the scummed scroll
Spells no legacy where the heaven-eyed
Invader draws love beyond the Fall.

My dream drained slowly to the blown tress
And the waking unscourged fingers: wave after wave
Of pleasure would interpret
My opened wealth. So there came to your parish
What old defiant Knox found in Margaret,
What Burns sought with tears at Mary's grave.

Joseph Hocking (1855-1937), Cornish novelist and Methodist minister, was a Terras tin-miner's son, a cousin of mine.

A Young Mystic

I *Goonamarris, 1933*

All very well for the gregarious Donne
To see mankind as solid, unified,
A mainland knocked by a common tide,
The whole mass robbed when death removed a stone.
But rare souls rise from rock-cells blown
From meteors, falling far out – solitaries,
Twisted spikes that snarl or shine alone.

I am poisonous crag; the thriving block rejects me:
The drill on its streets and mountains, the helm
In trade-brisk harbour and river,
Fulfil no itch or quest resembling mine.
My fellow men? The phrase is meaningless
When every ship that shuffles round my pillar
Bears flag and cargo of an unknown realm.
The upturned face is never of my species;
If any call or sign
Comes through gale or mist, it is foreign:
I bristle and flash and am at war.

I cannot be the norm, the human being
Fretted by fear of bombs or of the sack,
Vivid with friends, agreeing or disagreeing,
Thrilled with pride to see a Union Jack.
For me there is no union
Beyond the primal bonds of God and sex,
And these are so formed in me, so meteor-flaked,
That no one on the mainland, no one
On the trading decks, would guess
What I mean by the Name, what I seek in a kiss.

My lot's no part of suffering mankind,
For human ills throb through the whole mass,
Are understood and draw forth sympathy.
I think of the afflicted, deaf or blind
Or crippled: they remain inside

The general strata of human pain,
And their thirst is slaked
By the usual plaudit: they are not lonely
With my aloofness – that of a star-grain.

II *Goonamarris, 1940*

What growth could end the quarrel?
    Only the unique Rock
Where the mainland was exposed
    At the crow of a cock,
And in Peter's broken seam
    New love-cells could gleam.

How could love bridge the distance
    To my tongue of stellar pride?
The Source of all cells was there,
    Seeking mine for His Bride.
A church ray struck my base,
    Blessed the misfitting face.

How did I snap the selfhood
    That rasped at Peter's keys?
All fear of the trading craft
    Thawed in singing seas:
The Image that baulked my curse
    Courted the universe.

Josephine Butler

These brothel steps lead back to Mersey grime,
Gas-jets and a foul wind fretting the street,
Spidery shadows everywhere.
It's past midnight, the waiting-rooms are packed:
Troops, boys of eighteen....I have been inside,
Spoken to some of them, made contact
With girls tripping out to solicit.
My tears and prayers go burning into the slime,
The web that trails from the blood's tricked heat.
God, why do I dare –
I, married and fifty – defy the established crime?

While a million wives lie free, soothed with their husbands,
Unhaunted by harlots' laughter, in a sweet swell
Like that which cured my unstrung girlhood's
Acid of questions, I am driven to docks and stews,
To the soul's vicarious, bitterest black sands,
Where the urge of rescue receives the bruise
From the stony chattel, the cynical male stride,
The trafficker's manipulation
Of a State licence to buy and sell.
I lead my period's
Christ-war on vice, on a vast betrayal – England's.

I've fought the C.D. Acts and Bruce's Bill,
Morals police, the regulated sewer,
And apathy in decorous pews.
My life was sometimes threatened: brothel-keepers
Worked up the mob, set buildings ablaze. Still
I thrust at public conscience, gave lepers
The tender truth, slipping through the official
Cordon of steel-toned disgust
To bid Christ's martyred love conquer.
Fire in me cannot choose:
Pure flame would gut cruel threads, snap the last dark thrill.

A Night in Soho
(to John Donne)

That night in Soho – the only night
I ever spent in London – you
Towered, more awesome than the trite,
Though gracious, plaster saints I scarcely knew.
I had plumbed your weird cavern often, drawn
From my drained Wesleyan cell
Deep in clayscape, to your dark and dawn:
They freed me from my age, which spun the crossed shell
Or the hot phallic image in the neon-swell.

I had skirted bomb rubble, stumbling in
From the street to that Catholic boarding-house:
I felt the medieval terrors – sin,
Judgment and the worms' distilled carouse.
Only St Paul's, your intact stone
Tongue, chimed a post-war grace.
You hymned the whore's licence and the rake's bone,
Then blasted through to our time, to me in that place,
The art of a coping penitence, renewing the race.

I lay in bed, still a young man
Groping for love, and your shade towered
Among my thoughts of Cornwall, Ann,
And the cavern of truth where the new seeds flashed and flowered.
I knew I was following you: there were tears
I remembered, on a soft key –
Some dream-form of pure earth on which appears,
As Ann's full ardours showed you constantly,
Christ's Passion-mark, chilling the wit of our vanity.

I was soon whisked back to Paddington:
A city more pagan while I slept
Than when you preached, cried to the sun.
Had I alone shared your contrite gloom and kept
Your ray, with cold saints beside my bed?
Fierce battling sensualist,
For whom the bell tolled in the maidenhead,
And the Lamb's blood, at work in the carnal twist,
Raised the true ecstasy of the soul's alchemist!

121

Wessex and Lyonnesse

An hour before I stood on Bulbarrow
I watched the hermit Powys, ruddy and leonine,
Puff pipe-smoke musingly
Into a modest book-strewn room.
He had just soaked bread-and-butter in his tea,
Explaining that Jesus did
Something like that. But there was no Judas, no
Croak of fate's craft in the Dorset valley.
As I waved farewell through the clear notching sunshine
The Hardy-refuting peace was solid.

I felt exultant on the massive green brow
With High Stoy in haze, the bland Stour winding seaward
Through late summer's restful flourish of trees;
Yet I gleaned no hint of the true cause,
The destined link with my half-breathed romantic vow.

The breeze brought no quiver across Egdon
From a young heart labouring hiddenly
Down there beside the calm Channel –
Heart bruised by a knuckle of false tide
At the end of a cramped, pious tunnel.
Already, though unknown to me,
Her eyes were questioning the quiet palms
And the white chipped anvil, the Isle of Slingers,
Seeking, beyond ascetic laws,
Love's reborn shape that no iron cuts or hammers.

I soon turned back, reluctantly,
To a savage Cornwall – scoop's bite, earth-rind peeling,
Crashing in fetid lumps during night shifts,
Purged at pit-level or on a kiln-pan.
But a radiance stayed, played on the lanced and reeling
Loam: I was strangely mature, having lost all dark belief
In the chronic martyrdom of man.

I denied pit-torture, she the dusty prison,
For eighteen years more...
Now she prepares the hallowed meal

In a so-called hermit's modest book-strewn room
Down in Hardy's Lyonnesse.
But there is no sop, no Judas,
No croak of Fates or chorus of the Pities;
Only solid peace, out-pacing the martyr-season.

Whispers

These whispers must come from ahead,
From a point where the road bends round
Into faith-flushed terrain again,
Beyond the last factory-shed
Of secular mirage. They have haunted
Not merely my raw birth-dower
Of iron tracks, quarry-faces
And thin sand-scratching furze,
But palm and pebbly beach more fitly hers
Whose whisper warms, confirms their message.

To tire of current babble
Could not evoke such clear intimations
Unless something lived and moved, articulate
Outside the jarring circuit: without this,
My fret or boredom could bring only
The screwed frost of silence.

I am not tired: the whispers give me power,
Not insulating, sealing me in an archaic climate.
I have trudged the menaced and changeful way
Down through the twentieth century,
Smelt petrol, drugs and bleaching chemicals,
Passed supermarkets, laboratories, clinics.

I have heard men's voices barking on the moon,
Bomb-clouts and the shrieked pop tune;
Stood under excavators that baptised me
With rain from their poised dull teeth;
Seen white spoil-heaps, first conical, turn oblong,
And subtler crusts of thought turn sour.

I know what today's paper claims
For the birth pills, what some bishops preach
About a shrivelled God and shrivelling mortals,
And what young trendy poets write
Concerning urinals.
I have caught the dry jargon, watched the expert hands

Plaster neat labels on holy places,
Call the terrible secret of God a neurosis,
The terrible insights of sex an obsession.

The whispers that echo in my lines
Laugh gently among buds of the future,
For a wind will rise against the vulgar term,
And terror is truth in the intermediate
Regions between nullity and centre.

If flawed cells flared in the murmuring germ
Till I rasped and hurled rocks like a clay titan,
There is no regret on the lulled levels,
For they are private. The rebel's
Fire and peril remain; intense
Listening stiffens my rejection
Of the broad escape-route's signs.
Even her pebbly beach under the calm bran-
Coloured cliff borders the oolite quarries
Where stone was cracked to bear
A whispering gallery, like our faith's, ringed by nightmare.

Herman Melville

I searched through white death native
   And coloured life not native but showered
Amid the strange torments of my voyages
   Where thought-shells melted, vision grew blood-powered.

Coral and coconut and glittering dance –
   A hint of undraped priestliness, of Eden;
But I saw girls' naked brown breasts gnawed
   By the ulcerous lips of our whalemen.

A sewn shroud on the *Acushnet*'s deck
   Under the spume-flogged, venomous masts:
I felt a sea-monster heave at the hull;
   Within nature's storm, the unknown counterblasts.

Ultimate claimed a voice in me,
   In the obscure hunt and haunting:
I would see Christ's white tomb, sense Ahab's white whale
   Rise, bulk and vapour writhing.

From soft lagoons of the Marquesas,
   Where traders bring plague and our priests barrenly bow,
I brought a cry of seed and selfhood,
   Hurled at some force that shrouds my genius now.

Huge floundering rhythms came – no neat art,
   No nimble song on a harboured rigging:
My deeps, born dour as Ben Nevis,
   Were split by a mystic deluging.

I was husband and father, yet I echoed
   Whale-spout and archangel's horn.
Harpoons may still drift where my Southern saga
   Closed: I bled then from America's scorn.

That dark demented clash in remote waters
   Faded in cold ambiguity:
Would Christ slay pride of doubt or pride of faith
   Or pride of blood, or save, transform all three?

No clue, no settlement: the hideous wrangle
  Hardens the world. But I have withdrawn:
My wife the true surrendered island,
  The sole, frail hint of palm and throne.

St Gildas

(in tribute to Alexis Carrel)

Albatross, petrel, or a more fabulous bird
Might fitly watch him while he stands alone
On the shrunken cliff, that ageing, puzzling Carrel –
Monk-like and surgical,
Wrestling and detached, cautious and love-spurred.
The last splintered ardours of sunset
Sag past him to soften the mainland coast.

He scans the worn gaunt bones of his island home
And the dividing tide racing more swiftly,
Grinding louder as the night nears.
Fearlessly his mind and spirit
Probe on, knitting tissues of the unknown.

If weird bleak Brittany
Has Celtic ties with Cornwall, I care little.
Such roots are brief, twin stems of tongue and custom
Break on petty ground. No place can touch me
Until I know a great soul touched it,
Was torn, reborn there, threw on rock and tree,
On street or meadow-scene,
Some clue to the heaven-sowing presence, some sign of exit
From an untravailling routine.

I look towards St Gildas
Merely to honour a soul scarred and lonely –
This scientist and mystic, weaver of extremes,
Who trusts the curt rational data
And the flaming creed, reveres both chart and chant.

As he notes the imprisoned, moon-swayed toil of the sea
He recalls the Lourdes pools, stirred by the free, immaculate
Virtue of an unmapped star.
The open, unchilled truth is less distant,
Though the known cliff is cramped and crumbling.

Methods. Voices in the wind.
Dissect. Anoint.
The clash first, then the homeward fusion-point.

128

Wamba Convent 1964

Rebel soldiers! Oh Mary, here's Congo hell's
Heat, denser than we dreamed, inside the cloisters.
Brothel-glint, war custom, burst on our cells;
The scars of black tusks deface the ivory
When veil and habit are torn from us.
Turris eburnea,
Ora pro nobis.

Never again like your earthly body, gracious
Virgin unstained, will our once nun-null
Woman-forms curve and tremble at the Cross:
Towers we sealed for our shielding Bridegroom
Brute-shadows loot, quenching the candled kiss.
Turris eburnea,
Ora pro nobis.

Did you speak comfort through the English prisoner,
Not of our fold, wearing no crucifix,
But sharing our shame? She claimed, Mother,
No assault can spoil, soil Christ's bridal temple,
That more than soul stays pure in this abyss.
Turris eburnea,
Ora pro nobis.

True, there's no traffic here, no flesh-fire's
Sold or exchanged: perhaps the limb-locking vow
Need quail no more at rape than at death-virus.
A body Christ bought, mine, still whole?
Could spirit but show
Links, overlappings, where its real robe is!
Turris eburnea,
Ora pro nobis.

We came coifed against Congo's drumming arts,
Built our base, God's hidden forge in the forest.
How far the armour, the mystic woman-parts,
Cover us now is His secret, guessed
Dimly through anguish of involved senses.
Turris eburnea,
Ora pro nobis.

E

On the Burial of a Poet Laureate
(to C.D.L., May 1972)

Laureate, your heart rests, after a rainy Whitsun,
    Close to grave Hardy's heart which bore
Much the same toils: warrant of Western sunset,
The church towers fading, the unransomed moor
Thrusting the outcasts, stoic or Promethean,
    To sea's verge and poet's core.

You thrilled the psalm until the bells turned bitter
    On your sharp, copious mind:
Climate of revolution, honest thinking,
Shrivelled for you the long solace of mankind.
No mystic, you sought a basis newer, fitter,
    Down to the common grind.

You scanned the pylon, the bold tractor lurching,
    The bomb-gash on the town,
Found fuel awhile among the plotting comrades;
But there came storm and flight, with Red rhythms blown,
Silenced by Devon's thick dialect of suffering:
    Your spirit then groped alone.

I could join you there, in the discovery
    That the resinous craft,
Pure form, needs inward friction, the soul bowed, searching
For truths unchanged by sunset: not the draught
Or drive of mundane systems, but a crosstree,
    Grail-blood, the cosmic graft.

You told me once my firm and clarion metres
    Suspended your disbelief:
So rebel-rough, incisive, free from mildew
Was the faith erupting in me after brief
Tensions of darkness: you saw the mournful fetters
    Burst on my clay-pit reef.

What changed the climate on my gritty island,
  Kept me from faith's decline?
Two hearts, bereft and yearning, make Dorset soil
Nobler now and strangely nearer mine;
But rainless Whitsun nourishes my clay-land
  With an undimmed altar-sign.

Royal Wedding

Sun sparkles on London crowds, though here in the west
November fog sneaks round the dying shrub-stems
Outside one of England's humblest cottages:
A century old, blunt granite, and industrial rubble
Fumbling close by, with some garages.
We who live wedded here
Sit cleansed by Abbey music, fanfare,
And solemn voices flowing at the crest
Of another dream-drive among regal gems.

This is no hollow pomp, this is root and haven,
The sane oasis where hearts pause and listen
To the intoning tongue of half-forgotten springs,
The deep historic soundings
From the rock-base, at the courtly arrival.

Feel now, how mean and small
Is the modern desert, drably efficient,
Swept by sullen agitation
Where the grey waste meets the red sand!
We have feared the ignoble trampling
Set as tomorrow's march for our people;
The alien expanse with no gracious order,
No traditional command,
But only the raw rasp of gravelly bluster
And machine-geared instinct, blind through separation
From the silken splendour of a reverent vow.

Bones of great lovers lie in this oasis:
Browning and Tennyson, who showed what the English meant
By marriage: rose-flush in a hushed garden,
Sheath of oak-shade, massive and wholesome,
Folding the plain vein, a pledge
Of ancient power and knowledge,
Northern and Christian. We need this
Revived, need voices to restore the flow,
Spread the crowned wisdom, let the chanting
Waters redeem the dry furrow.

A Wife on an Autumn Anniversary

Much to sort out: rending rain on screes,
Sun-strut, prick of mists,
Thunder on tin tabernacles,
Moon-glide on cavern votaries,
And the moralist's
Dilemma between keys and shackles.

But I know the weather and the gate
That called and fitted
The woman I am – love's witness shy
Among your psalming leaves. I can state
When falsehood quitted
And the residue summed our earth and sky.

Decades of treading in shifts of air
That left scorch-print or frostbite
At bolted or gaping entrances.
Few were authentic, though hearts share,
Through flood-terror at night
And noon's stare at ruin, some nakedness.

Not the highest, not this where your leaves veil me
And I trace the true lines back
To sprays of glad weather on a palmy outpost,
My body sensing the unwarped key.
Tin and stone grew black
In storm – love's vision dead almost.

Tragic depth takes a spurious turn,
And the haggard lesson
Must be unlearned in the ripe, safe coupling.
My first desire at the beaded cavern
Matched sun-wooed screes: you won
Against false weather on your sapling.

Five years with your positive bright leaves!
I, too, hear the rumour
Scraped on the autumn vein: we meet
Pain in a new context. Our earth grieves
Within the golden humour
Rayed from soul's heaven's unshifting heat.

Tregargus

A rainbow, like my vesper, arches down
Towards the nibbling waterfall,
And a Cornish valley, enduring its grey doom
Of mundane infiltration, is revived and hooded,
Or crowned rather, with a soft bardic signal.

A stream was diverted so that the pitched grit,
Clay-waste, could crawl and swell on the natural bed,
But the crooked current still arrives and plashes
With a pattering hum over the stubborn boulders,
Hissing a mellowing in the ravine;
And a pipe-line bears the warm, invisible mica
Past scratching hollies in the cleft wood.

Some roofless sheds or clay-dries
Crumble amid trees and small wild fruit
On which poisonous powder, flakes of blown lime,
Preach their wan parable:
This was an evening without issue, husked
Where clammy trenches cut the track dead.

The ravine bends round to a stone-mill:
In boyhood I saw its big wheel flinch,
Stumble down, scrubbed by the pounding trough-torrent,
And the crushed stone was seed-like and sterile
Behind the blind grey wall.

But the soft coloured arch bends, potent now
As my vesper, for grey is refused
At the source of the bardic span
The waterfall's thrum is mesmeric,
Half-sad, yet matching the rainbow, the curve
Of a song diverted, reaching us after the blast.

FROM **A DIFFERENT DRUMMER**
(1986)

Poem at Sixty

So many poets, before they reached three-score,
Let their despair employ a coroner.
As the March rain now hammers
The slate above my birth-room, I recall a few:
Chatterton, Beddoes, Davidson, Mew,
Hart Crane, Vachel Lindsay...I think my stars
Were as tragic as theirs, yet my pen
Still throws up clues to my survival,
A massed chorus with no broken bars.

The hill-setting has changed wickedly for the worse:
The daily slobber of spawned crystals
Creeps nearer my windows, blocking the view
Of grassy dome, wood and pasture
Which in infancy I watched with vague wonder,
And in youth with glum indifference
As my inner life submerged, feeling the scabs of the outcast
More true than the comforting green.

Lorry-tracks and footpaths have multiplied
Around the marooned home walls,
Twisting past sheds, dumps, mica-beds,
Where cows grazed when I took my first stride
Towards public fire. The tracks of my nature,
Subtly linking the crossing, were always lonely,
Unsponsored, misjudged, hardly Cornish at all.
Nowhere between Land's End and Tamar
Had a pen-stroke left a mark that guided my steps
Or cut a kindred passage.

Romantic sentiment – squires and halls,
Prudent ideals, academic precision –
What could these mean to me
Who needed the unschooled artist's crucible,
The revivalist's platform, the hermit's cell,
The theologian's tome open on granite, open to upland winds,
And the sex-mystic's pulse of moon-tokens on the loyal
Pressed lips and breasts? For almost half a century
I was so many selves in one skin

That the entangled contending veins
Would have snapped in early frost
Had I not found a unifying trust.

My character, like the scarred plateau
That bore me, had its geometry askew –
Lopped, slanted, swollen: the crystal peaks
Craned in a barren patchwork till, beyond art,
Outside the blood's moods and the mind's,
I found scope and motive in the far call
Rising through mother's and wife's prayer, breaking despair.

Louder than the sea that silenced Davidson,
Stronger than the poison that ended Lindsay's twang,
The old Damascus call brought me balance.
All my gifts straightened and tasted sweet
As the glib exhibit ceased to be the norm of advance
And the brooding ego the norm of retreat.

In Roche Church

Inland now, though soon to tread sea-sand again,
We kneel alone in the cool hill-top church,
Screened from Hensbarrow clay-smirch,
Guarded by clean pillars, free to marvel
At the way we ride the grey test, long past our vow.
Didn't the autumn winds howl warning
Of an ill-equipped and ill-timed venture in the wrong
Climate? Yet the calm tower
Is apt above our private gesture,
And the altar's mystery breathes through the centuries' dust
As her arm, eight years familiar, presses my waist.

There's a famous freak rock near us,
A black savage skull of a thing on the moor.
Monks built a chapel there and one wall stands
Facing the sea still, high on the schorl mass.
Gales from both coasts have struck the pinnacle
A thousand times, and shaken this church door
Which we approached under fragrant leafage
Up the lane from a July-scorched stile...
Something remains impregnable, holds evidence
Without a technique of defence.

Nimble cliff-climb up the crumbling stone stairs,
That we find true safety when storm knocks at night
Along our tissue of coast, swamping cave and landmark.
No: that's the cunning animal dodge,
Not for monks or the deeply married.
We must show man's stature, massive as the floundering assault;
We must cease to sharpen our wits
In training for trivial exits.

Man's way – our way at least – is a faith transcendent,
Hammered by storms from birth, clumsily sculptured,
Often seeming an obtuse image,
Neither skilled nor frantic when the boat splits
Or the tide traps, yet always preserved.
Nobody knows how. We are too intent
On the unseen touch, angel's wing, communion with a soul-mate,

To care whether our rescued feet
Tread sand or rock or moorland spur
Or the paved church. A random whim
Of unforced reverence has made us kneel,
Heads bowed, awed by our love's survival.

Drought on a Clay Ridge

The slopes look drained and old, passive as Egypt,
Though the hot pyramids are white mineral waste
And the insects are still English.
A freak tropic climate has been testing
The wrong fibres and the wrong blood: all's in collapse.
Tired worried eyes watch a mummified landscape,
The natural bits of it gone brown or yellowish
Long before autumn. Not a shoot of pure green
Breathes on the baked clods or between the dazed stones.

I can't recognise my own garden hedge:
It's all straw – or more like a heap of shavings,
Crisp, loosely packed, unlike a rooted substance,
Unlike normal grass in winter.
Nothing here has had its day:
Wizard weather brought wizened stillbirths;
The sap's leap was stunned by the rainless grin overhead.

I loved to tilt the strong foxglove cups,
So sleek amid the rough leaves, here in summer.
But this year they did not open:
Small deformed skins tried to thicken,
But were scorched dry, shrunk like tissue-paper
And dropped in shreds from dead, rigid stems.

Almost daily, in lanes that sweat tar,
A fire-engine clangs and rattles through dust-clouds,
Through odours from over-heated walls and wood,
Racing to a field or down-patch
Where something that should drip sap is ablaze.

The smoke does not rise or spread fast
In the compressed atmosphere:
It huddles and thins around the absurd commotion
Till the weary, exasperated firemen
Are back on the road again, heading for more trouble
From the bland incendiary sun,
Leaving another black sore where the soot's
A shameful substitute for bloom and berry.

Weird and desolate in a new way
Are the mine-scarred hills, the pyramid-shadowed valleys:
The native feels himself a foreigner
When the climate disregards his roots.

Jim Elliot

Rugged wrestler, Wheaton-trained, tough as Hemingway,
He saw life stripped and God-raided;
His look was gay or thunder-shaded
As the beckoning hibiscus by the Curaray.

He tore himself loose from culture; a sinewy flame
Lit his raw track to the Absolute.
Truth peeled was truth beyond dispute:
He hacked through convention to the bare cloven Name.

Religionless faith, more radical than Bonhoeffer's,
Blazed its challenge through his hard grip:
Unmoved amid civilised worship,
He strained for a fall where the wild tangle suffers.

The single outer Word, printed or prayer-caught,
Guided and sealed stubbornly
Decisions that gave sheer agony
To his male roots when storming nature brought

Thrust of love's bloom and the Voice said 'Sacrifice'.
He scorned the pseudo-mystic stuff:
'The secular is sacred enough;
The God within must bid the sweet sap rise.'

He cried: 'I'm mad for her, God, but I'll obey
Your opening call from a mud floor
In the sweating jungle of Ecuador.'
Yet he was no monk, sailing south with this price to pay.

Five years of abstinence, unappeased desire,
Witness to omnipotent law,
Objective mandate checking his flaw
Of self-fulfilment: still he prayed for her.

The test-ground was stark and lurid: frenzy of bull-fights,
River floods, danger from boa, puma,
Mosquito: he fought malaria,
Heard Indians scream, drowning or dying of snake-bites.

The will, the principle, never the personal instinct,
Based his sure steps till he saw truth's dawn
Change Quichua faces as love shone
In dark tribal eyes; then the denied dream linked

With the ripe phase of the mandate. Orchid and coffee-palm
Brushed the beloved: she was at his hut,
At the crest of her Kingdom vision that shut
For so long the earth-pulse from the spirit's psalm.

Their sanctions, as rebel pioneers, allowed
No room for a churchy marriage service:
God and a drab old Quito office
Rebuked the hollow shows. And when Elliot bowed

On the Curaray airstrip, pierced by the lance of an Auca,
Martyred for making Christ his chief,
A twin faith rebuked the clouding grief
In the woman clasping his child at Shandia.

*Jim Elliot, a rebel American missionary, was
murdered in Ecuador in 1956.*

Mappowder Revisited

(to Gerard Casey)

The old Powys lodge is barred to us:
Fable and litany have gone from it
Since I alighted, young, warm from a dusty car,
And met the hermit at the lounge window. I touch it now,
Gravely, knowing he died here, calm in a russet-leaf fall,
Rebuking our century.

I could see behind him the arched doorway,
Slightly blurred but accessible to me
Even without guidance. My inward eye,
Which had borne so much Venus-white pit-glare,
Welcomed the portal dusk, the rich bursting land.

Intense rural smells are still the same –
Horses, thatch, the immoderate summer perfume
Of banqueting trees and flowers...
There was a feast, a crest of prevision,
A veil rent amid the mixed odours.
I had long cherished, from a different angle,
His picture of a God, who was not Pan,
Moving among the virgins.

In this hour of vindication,
When the lodge is too bitter-sweet,
We pass on to the churchyard,
Small and mellow, just a few steps up the lane.

I bend over the Powys tombstone:
Smooth curve of the carved book,
Rough inscription, meaning only a marriage
And two deaths.

We are reverent, feeling the pulse
Of a marriage and two lives;
And for us, as for that strange hermit,
The heart is in the pew, the cool humble station
Which means listening and communion
Till a sunshaft finds the golden Cross.

Gaze on the mystery, as he gazed
After his pen dried, and you have the clue
To my presence again in Dorset.

I would not return with the gleam unfulfilled,
For a poet's debauch of nostalgia and lamentation.
Sitting beside my partner in Powys' pew,
I share the great silence
Of earth at evening and heaven timeless – both totally real.

T.F. Powys, novelist, and story writer, abandoned literature for a life of mystic meditation and retired to the rectory lodge at Mappowder, Dorset, in 1940. I visited him there in 1950, and in 1978 my wife and I stood at his grave in Mappowder churchyard.

Sandsfoot Castle Gardens

Damp-haired in the stone memorial shelter,
We sit while a shower veils Portland harbour
And the palms look strange, marking no oasis,
Rejecting the desert image, since their fruits,
Like the buds of the neighbouring rose-bowers, swell
Between the cove and suburban Rodwell.

Along the railings of the Tudor castle,
Now a ruined fort, the new drops run,
Abreast of today's history –
Our history even, freed from siege and dungeon
And the monastic relics filched, misplaced
When our royal goal could not be traced.

Soft Channel rain glides, too, from the slim green banners
Hoisted by sap on the live ringed pillars,
The palm trunks. You watch the leaves dance,
While I recall white crystals and the red
Fanatic tinge on humped hills as dawn broke,
Etching a scraggy thorn-clump. How different here, instead,
Is the push of the delicate palm-roots,
Strong and confident through dense English earth,
With no shift and cackle of dry grains,
No whirlwind on a scorching horizon.

Outside, near the steps, the naked sundial
Has ceased to show the hour: it's a graven stump,
But not a silent sphinx. It was warm with sun
When we passed it, and it spoke,
Not of time but the unshadowed smile.

I have questioned often, questioned the worth
Of the long pain and mirage, the rotten clay-fields,
Or the cruel fate distorting clay-fields and me.
I hardly care where the blame goes:
Five pattering minutes more
And we shall caress together
The laughing tongue of the palm tree,
The damp full lip of the rose.

In a Truro Garden
(to Margaret Shirley)

A summer hour of infinite scope,
Pulse and patchwork restful – path, mown slope,
Hot slant on neck, brow, right cheek or left
As I turn at her supple urge,
Then tunnel-feeling, eclipse, cool draught,
Stiff boughs scraping till we emerge.

We stoop at a sleepy pool's rim,
Touch wet stone – I fancy the gleam
Quiver, get quenched by cloud-shifts;
Then it's flower-shapes at my finger-ends –
Winged, grooved or studded: a petal lifts,
Rough and spongy, a smooth tip bends.

Now, higher up, we're in the orchard:
Pleasant to feel my forehead
Nudged by a living apple,
A fruit still fed among leaves,
In sight of the slim clear grey cathedral
Which answers the bad fruit – Eve's.

It's a spreading answer, we can tell:
The vines thrive here on the wall;
There's an unclogged scent, a sunning cat –
No scare from a serpent's hiss,
No sylvan treason. Across the flat
Flushed tongue of our city the spires spill bliss.

*This poem describes a visit my wife and I paid
to the home and old-world garden of Mrs Shirley
at Vean, near Truro Cathedral, in the 1970s.*

Chesil Beach

My feet tread the fragmented crust,
Slipping between enormous pebbles massed
In salty dyke-piles above the checked flow
That crawls and cranes through crannies, its Channel-powered jabs
Dislodging some lower slabs
With a dull submerged rattle. The miles-long heap
Has no angles or splinters: the pebbles, fawn or grey,
Shine smooth, rounded like eggs, stacked in shrill profusion
Near the dignified west curve of Weymouth Bay.

I am no foreigner here
If one can judge by an atmosphere.
This is my birth-image – freak and chaos,
A stammer of stone where custom called for sand,
The hard proud lump where you'd expect glued grains
Meek in a flat dough of convention.
A wilful breach of geological rules
Is pleasing to one who has evaded schools,
Sought the rare pattern, the fantastic stress,
The awkward blessing on the soul's isthmus.

I do not lurch on these stones alone:
She who gaily slithers beside me
Has long observed the tide's strange focus
And drawn comfort from seeing it barred
Where the tarred causeway, the quick friendly headlights,
Relieve the dusk-harsh gabble and rinsing.

We're on the Portland side – the Isle of Slingers
With its high-walled, efficient jail.
A tide has entered there, made some stones ring:
We were privileged guests with the singers,
The guitar-throb in the prison chapel
Where the convicts are rounded. Freak and chaos
Were the criminals' heritage and mine,
Since we were not of docile grain;
Only, for some reason, I am free
To come back here, taste human love's vivacity
And innocently scramble
From primeval pebbles to the brisk normal road.

Eilidh Boadella

Night sky as Keats saw it
Over at Lulworth, but here the shore
Is a mass of clanking loose-jointed armour,
With the dark sea springing to claw it.
The girl sits on a restless, faintly rattling ridge,
Dim in starshine, her waist-length hair
Tugged and tossed like her invaded spirit.

The waves whisper, 'Millions of children starve';
The pebbles rasp, 'Some children have abortions;
They didn't stay starved long enough,
And they forgot the pill.'
Cruel confusion, a world's woe breaking in
Too soon on the tender nerve.
She murmurs, 'I must empty myself, I must serve.'

Her poet-fibre withstands
Briefly, clinging to beauty.
'Bright star, enchant my Dorset still…
No, I am beyond, I am dedicated.
Bright star, would I were constant as
Mother Teresa's helpers in Calcutta.

'The foul streets sweat, the creeping shadows are callous.
Lift the dustbin lid: there's a baby inside,
Its brown skin smelling of scabs.
We'll snatch and rescue…My hands
Must do more than stroke these Chesil slabs:
So few get the vision – so few.'

Abbotsbury holds some African trees
In its tropical gardens, up there on the hill.
'Black children are dying in famines, massacres:
I feel these smooth stones turn to splinters
Of human bones. My head has shed
Dream-ground that spilled glib rhymes
Over flowers' tints and birds' trilling.
How can these self-fulfilling
Poets live with their conscience?
I must answer the wider homecall.

'Bright star, Lulworth way,
Goodbye! Brighter star,
Bethlehem way, empty me of all.'

Eilidh Boadella was a young Dorset poet whose verse was published posthumously in
I Won't Paint any Tears *(Outposts, 1981). She had a profound religious experience which
made her choose a life of poverty and sacrifice. She died in a fire at a London Mother Teresa
hostel in March 1980.*

NEW POEMS

Open Waters

A slap of spray on my left ear
Makes me rub salt drops off my neck
And feel proud of my drenched collar.
The motor-launch quivers and tilts
At the heavier wave-banks. I lean overboard,
Pull a rope, shift with the unrhythmic roll,
Glad I've never been seasick,
And hardly attuned to an awareness
That I live in a sick world.

The pleasure-boat noses near
Warships, helicopters, the bleak naval base;
Portland prison squats glum on the cliff.
But our innocent craft, moored elsewhere
Last night, chugs safe and unshadowed.

Weather experts have told us
We breathe poisoned air – some nuclear leak.
I hazily take it – the snag
Of a warped breed's invention;
But this gusty wind, if poisoned, still feels fine,
And my wife laughs, forgetting the warning.

I think of another dimension –
A Dissent hub on a Weymouth quay,
An open baptistry, wet hair on my cheek;
And I touch the unquenched praise
Believers have always smuggled
Into a world ever menaced, yet intact.

Leaks of evil brought those convicts
To the drab rot of the cells;
Battleships scar our view of Sandsfoot
Because of poisoned politics.
But our pleasure-boat still dances
Like the affirming heart, the outreach
From the hymn-tongued immersion, till this leaking spray
Links me with the exempt waters.

Palazzo Rezzonico

(for Benedict and Lilah)

Was there ever, in medieval Italy,
A more incredible wizardry? This whim and whisk
Of Providence peeled a foreign fate,
Breaking the dull smeared chrysalis,
Teaching a trick of levitation,
Air-flight at seventy-one, till the unclayed body
Boarded a gondola at Venice.

Canal-veined city: its golden heart now beats
Congruous to my new destiny,
Naming the broad sea, the split channels
Unstained by fevers of cramped history.
I sense, in this enchantment,
Not Doges and Shylocks but the gain
Of a soul's voyage to the point furthest out
From its natural source and scent
And the landmarks of the home-taught brain.

Back in Cornwall, remote from these flowing streets,
My Bridge of Sighs was an unfenced plank
Above the clay-slime. I felt giddy,
But even in my hermit-bonds prepared to thank
God for what native wit called mirage.

I clung, by stubborn grace, to the alien
Glitter of the Browning pattern
Which closed here, noble and clean,
Near the reserved church, in a frescoed palace.

Wedding allegory on a ceiling
Spills clues to the room of homage,
High over the nodding gondolas
And the whispering water's affirmation
Of outreach, the ultimate glad bridge.

Jean-Pierre de Caussade

He went blind at seventy or so,
Groped for candles and the holy cup
In the bristling Jesuit house
He had guided firmly at Toulouse;
And no one guessed that his eyes once led a quill
On lengthy excursions in a cramped cell
To reap his pale, prayer-battered insights.
His book remained anonymous
For a century, feeding a mystic flow
In his confrères and some Quietists.

Age and the quenched rainbow set me
Near him, but my human probe
Flared far from his placid theory
About an equal influx of divine love
At every moment, making the present impact
The only one now valid and heaven-charged.
Rather, grace soothes my opaque flats of fact,
During the test-hour, from past heights
Of the senses' sunniest ardour.

We poets seldom shine at contemplation
Or monkish meditation:
I am rare, for I stress prayer
And, like Jean-Pierre, know the purged soul's delights,
But the ties, the tides, the tidings do not tally.
The ascetic hint from uncomfortable mists
Seems a scurrilous thorn to me, chiding my praise
For a secure day's
Teeming caress and the sea-foam on her hair.

Index of Titles and First Lines

Jack Clemo was born in 1916 near St Austell, Cornwall. Son of a clay-kiln worker, he received only a village school education, but devoted himself entirely to writing throughout a restless adolescence. He remained a mystical recluse during his twenties, living in poverty with his widowed mother.

His first published novel, *Wilding Graft*, won an Atlantic Award in Literature from Birmingham University in 1948. An allegorical novel, *The Shadowed Bed*, which he wrote soon afterwards, was eventually published in 1986. He is the author of two volumes of autobiography, *Confession of a Rebel* (1949) and *Marriage of a Rebel* (1980), and a record of personal faith, *The Invading Gospel* (1958).

His first collection of poems, *The Clay Verge*, appeared in 1951, and was incorporated in a larger volume, *The Map of Clay*, ten years later. *The Wintry Priesthood*, a sequence which won an Arts Council Festival of Britain poetry prize in 1951, was also printed in *The Map of Clay*. Four other collections of poetry followed: *Cactus on Carmel* (1967), *The Echoing Tip* (1971), *Broad Autumn* (1975) and *A Different Drummer* (1986). He was awarded a Civil List pension in 1961, and a honorary D.Litt degree from Exeter University in 1981.

Although he had become blind and deaf in 1955, Jack Clemo married a Dorset woman, Ruth Peaty, in 1968, and in 1984 he and his wife left Cornwall and settled permanently in Weymouth.